ADULT ONLY PUB JOKES

Guaranteed to make you giggle!

HB

HINKLER
BOOKS

Joke Compilation: Scribblers and Writers
Cover Design: Sam Grimmer
Illustrations: John Shakespeare
Editor: Jasmine Chan
Typesetting: Midland Typesetters, Maryborough, VIC, Australia

 Adults Only Pub Jokes
First published in 2004 by Hinkler Books Pty Ltd
17-23 Redwood Drive
Dingley VIC 3172 Australia
www.hinklerbooks.com

First printed in 2004
Reprinted 2005

ISBN 1 7412 1656 7

Printed and bound in Australia

INTRODUCTION

I t's a place of madness, the microcosm of society. It's the pub, where all sorts of characters meet and all sorts of strange things happen.

Farmers, hookers, salesmen, bikies, you name it, they'll be in the pub, causing mayhem and being the source of plenty of belly laughs.

The pub is not only the place to tell jokes, but the place where jokes are created.

So let's celebrate the pub and its great contribution to society—not only do you get a drink there, but a good belly laugh, too!

ANIMALS AND PUBS

A polar bear walks into a pub. He sits at the bar and says to the barman, 'I'll have a gin ……………… and tonic, thanks.'
The barman replies, 'Why the big pause?'

A crocodile walks into a bar. The barman says, 'Why the long face . . .?'

A n old lady is proudly walking her poodle as she approaches a grimy pub.
As she passes the entrance a drunk stumbles out and vomits all over her dog.
'That's disgusting!' cries the lady.
'Struth,' says the drunk, 'It sure is. I can't remember eating that!'

A grasshopper goes into a bar. The barman says, 'Hey, we've got a cocktail named after you.'

The grasshopper replies, 'What? Greg?'

An echidna walks into a pub. He grabs the paper, takes a seat and starts browsing the sports pages.

The bartender, quite shocked, pours a beer for the echidna.

The little marsupial gives him a ten dollar note.

The barman figures, 'Here's a chance.' He hands over only one dollar change. The echidna says nothing.

After a little while, the echidna finishes his beer and goes to the bar to order another. The barman says, 'Y'know, we don't often get echidnas drinking here.'

To which the echidna says, 'I'm not surprised at nine dollars for a bloody beer!'

A girl at the pub asks the barman if he'll give her a free drink if she shows him something he's never seen before.

The barman agrees, so the girl pulls a guinea pig from her backpack.

She puts the little rodent on the bar and it begins to dance while singing 'All Night Long', by Lionel Richie.

The barman is blown away and gives the girl her free drink.

She then asks the barman if he'll give her another drink if she shows him something even more amazing. He agrees.

She pulls a frog and a small piano from her bag.

The frog croons The Beatles song 'Let it Be', while the guinea pig accompanies him on the piano.

The barman, flabbergasted, hands over another drink.

A barfly, who has witnessed the performance, sidles up to the girl and offers $1000 for the frog.

The girl agrees to the deal and sells him the frog.

'You're crazy!' says the barman, 'You could have made a fortune from that frog!'

The girl leans towards the barman, 'Don't say anything,' she whispers, 'but the guinea pig's a ventriloquist.'

A horse walks into a bar and asks for a bit to eat . . .

A termite walks into a bar and says, 'Is the bartender here?'

This guy walked into a bar with a large frog perched on his head.

'Where the hell did you get that?' asked the barman.

'Well,' the frog replied, 'You won't believe it, but it started out as this little wart on my ass!'

There were three pigs.

The first pig went to a bar, ordered a drink and gulped it down and went to the bathroom and then left.

The second pig went to the same bar, ordered a drink and gulped it down and went to the bathroom and then left.

The third pig went to the same bar, ordered a drink and gulped it down and was just going to leave, when the bartender asked if he was going to the bathroom. The third little pig said, 'No, I'm the little pig that goes wee wee wee, all the way home.'

A snail slid into a bar and ordered a beer.

The bartender said, 'Get out, you're a snail.' And he picked up the snail, threw him out of the door and across the street.

Eleven months later, while collecting glasses, the bartender felt a tap at his ankle.

The snail said, 'What the hell did you do that for?'

A pony walks into a bar and says, 'Bartender, may I have a drink?'

The bartender says, 'What? I can't hear you. Speak up!'

'May I please have a drink?'

'What? You have to speak up!'

'Could I please have a drink?'

'Now listen, if you don't speak up I will not serve you.'

'I'm sorry, I'm just a little hoarse . . .'

Three animals in a bar were having a huge argument over who was the best.

The first animal, a hawk, claimed that because of his ability to fly, he could attack anything repeatedly from above and that his prey had hardly a chance.

The second, a lion, based his claim on his strength. No one in the jungle dared to challenge him, King of the Jungle.

The third, a skunk, insisted he needed neither flight nor strength to frighten off any creature with his unique arsenal.

As the three debated the issue, a crocodile came in and swallowed them all, hawk, lion and stinker!

An armadillo walks into a bar, he goes to the counter and asks the barman, 'Have you seen my brother?'

The barman asks 'What does he look like . . .?'

An echidna walks into a bar and says that he'd like something to drink.

'Okay,' says the bartender. 'How about a beer?'

'N-o-o-o-o-o-o-o-o-o-o,' replies the echidna.

'Then how about a gin and tonic?'

'No-o-o-o-o-o-o-o-o-o.'

'A martini?'

'No-o-o-o-o-o-o-o-o-o.'

Finally, the bartender gets fed up and says, 'Hey, listen buddy, if you don't mind me asking—why the long "nos"?'

The bloke was an inveterate drunk.

His doctor was talking to him about the evil effects of demon drink and, in order to scare him into reforming his ways, suggested that the more he drank the smaller he would become.

'In the end you will become so small that you will turn into a mouse!' the doctor said.

The drunk went home and said to his wife, 'Darling, if you notice me getting smaller and smaller, will you kill the friggin' cat . . .'

THE BARMAN

A barman is doing the afternoon shift at a city bar. It's very quiet and the barman has little to do.

At ten past five, the local doctor comes in and orders an almond daiquiri.

They chat pleasantly and the doctor enjoys his drink.

The next day, at ten past five the doctor enters the bar and again orders an almond daiquiri. They again chat and all goes well.

The doctor becomes such a reliable regular that on his arrival, at ten past five, every day the barman has his almond daiquiri prepared and slams it on the bar as the doctor takes his seat.

One day, at a bit after five the barman realises that he is fresh out of almond. He rummages through his ingredients and finds some hickory essence and decides it'll have to do.

The doctor arrives at the usual time and takes his seat. The barman plonks the drink in front of him.

Slowly, the doctor raises the glass and takes a whiff.

'This is not an almond daiquiri,' he proclaims.

'No,' says the barman, 'It's a hickory daiquiri, Doc.'

A guy in a tie at a bar starts talking into his hand as if it were a phone.

The barman raises an eyebrow and goes up to the guy.

'Look mate, I don't know what the hell you're doing but it's weird and maybe you should go do it somewhere else.'

The guy in the tie explains, 'Oh, sorry but I'm a hi-tech businessman and I've had a phone implanted in my hand so I don't have to carry it around.'

The barman doesn't buy this, so the guy puts his hand to the barman's ear.

The barman has a quick chat to someone at the end of the line then apologises to the guy in the tie.

Halfway through his drink the guy in the tie heads for the men's room. He doesn't come out for some time.

The barman, fearing for the guy, eventually goes to check on him.

He finds the guy in the tie spread-eagled against the wall, pants down with toilet paper hanging out his arse.

'Oh no. What happened? Did they rob you?' asks the barman.

The guy replies, 'No, no. I'm okay. Just waiting for a fax.'

A man in a pub says to the barman, 'I'll bet you ten bucks I can bite my own ear.' The barman agrees to the wager. The man then pulls out his false teeth and bites his ear.

The barman bitterly hands over the money.

The man then says, 'I'll bet you 20 bucks I can lick my own eye.'

The barman, certain that the man can't have a false tongue, agrees to the bet.

The man pops out his glass eye, gives it a lick and pops it back in. The barman, frustrated, gives him a 20.

The man says, 'Alright, I'll give you a chance to get your money back.'

'See that empty glass at the end of the bar? I bet you $30 I can piss in it from here without spilling a drop.'

The barman agrees, knowing the task is impossible. The man drops his pants and starts pissing on the bar, on the floor, all over the bottles, in the peanuts and on the barman.

When he's done he hands the barman his money. The barman asks, 'What's that about? You just gave up your winnings.'

The man replies, 'Yep, but I bet those three guys at that table $100 each that I could piss all over you and your bar and you wouldn't mind.'

Chuck walked into the bar and proclaimed: 'I'm the best shot this town has ever seen.'

'Prove it,' said the bartender.

'See that guy playing the piano over in the corner?' said Chuck.

'Yep,' said the bartender.

'See his hat?'

'Yep.'

Chuck drew his pistol and shot the hat off the piano player's head.

Next day Chuck walked in again, still loudly proclaiming he was the best shot in town.

'Prove it,' said the bartender.

'See that guy in the corner playing the piano?'

'Yep.'

'See the cigarette in his mouth?'

'Yep.'

Chuck drew his pistol and shot the cigarette out of the piano player's mouth.

Next day, Chuck bounced into the bar again. 'I'm the best shot in town,' he shouted.

'You mind showing me your gun,' said the bartender.

Chuck handed over his gun. The bartender inspected it.

'Hmm,' he said. 'I reckon you should smear the barrel with Vaseline,' he said.

'Vaseline?' said Chuck. 'What for?'

'Well,' said the bartender. 'See that guy playing the piano over in the corner? His name's Wyatt Earp.

'And in a moment he's gonna come straight over here and shove that gun right up your arse.'

An armless man walked into a bar, which was empty except for the bartender.

He ordered a drink and when he was served, asked the bartender if he would get the money from his wallet in his pocket, since he had no arms.

The bartender obliged him.

He then asked if the bartender would tip the glass to his lips.

The bartender did this until the man finished his drink.

He then asked if the bartender would get a hanky from his pocket and wipe the foam from his lips.

The bartender did it and commented it must be very difficult not to have arms and have to ask someone to do nearly everything for him.

The man said, 'Yes, it is a bit embarrassing at times. By the way, where is your restroom?'

Without blinking, the bartender replied, 'The closest one is in the petrol station three blocks down the street . . .'

A young fella runs into a bar and says to the bartender, 'Give me 20 shots of your best scotch and make it quick!'

The bartender pours out the shots and the guy drinks them as fast as he can.

The bartender remarks, 'I've never seen anybody drink that fast!'

The lad replies, 'Well, you'd drink that fast too if you had what I have.'

'What do you have?' asks the bartender.

'Fifty cents!'

WHAT ON EARTH . . .?

A piece of string walks into a bar. He sits down but the barman says, 'Sorry mate, we don't serve string here.'

The disgruntled piece of string leaves the bar.

After a while the piece of string re-enters wearing sunglasses and a hat.

The barman says, 'Look sorry, but I know it's you and we don't serve pieces of string here. You'll have to leave.'

The piece of string ambles out.

He goes down the nearest lane, ties up one of his ends and rubs it against a brick wall. He re-enters the bar.

The barman, fed up, yells 'Look buddy, you know the rules now are you a piece of string or aren't you?'

To which the reply comes, 'I'm a frayed knot . . .'

A man walks into a bar. KLUNK.

A man walks into a bar with a roll of tarmac under his arm and says, 'I'll have a pot thanks and one for the road.'

A hat flies into a bar and rests on a stool.

He asks, 'Could I have a whisky please?'

The barman replies 'Look mate, your already off yer head.'

An eyeball rolls up to the bar and asks the barman for a brandy and dry.

The barman returns, 'Buddy, sorry, but I can't serve you. You're off yer face.'

Three vampires pop into their local pub. The first says, 'I'd like a pint of blood.'

The second says, 'Yeah, I'll have a pint of blood too.'

The third says, 'I'll have a pint of plasma.'

The barman says, 'Right. Let me get this straight. You want two bloods and a blood light?'

A jumper lead walks into a pub and orders a bourbon and coke. The barman says, 'Look mate, I'll serve you . . . but don't start anything.'

Two guys walk into a bar, but the third one ducked . . .

An Indian, a Rabbi, the Pope, an Aussie and an Irishman all walk into a bar together.

The bartender looks at all five of them quizzically and says, 'What is this . . . some kind of joke?'

Two cartons of yoghurt walk into a bar.

The bartender says to them, 'We don't serve your kind in here.'

One of the yoghurt cartons says back to him, 'And why not? We're cultured individuals.'

Two aliens were sitting in a bar.

Then one went 'Shabagoemdallada.' The other one says, 'Shut up Ralph you're drunk!'

A Number 12 walks into a bar and asks the barman for a pint of beer.

'Sorry I can't serve you,' states the barman.

'Why not?' asks the Number 12 with anger showing in its voice.

'You're under 18,' replies the barman.

C harles Dickens walks into a bar and orders a martini. The bartender asks, 'Olive or twist?'

WOMEN AND DRINK

Two women sit at a bar.
One of them asks the barman, 'Can I have a glass of wine for my friend?'

'Red or white,' asks the barman.

'Doesn't matter . . . she's colour blind.'

Once there was a beautiful woman whose two great joys in life were having a few drinks with a very good friend and working in her vegetable garden.

However, no matter what she did, she couldn't get her tomatoes to ripen.

She admired her friend's garden, which had beautiful bright red tomatoes.

One day while having a few drinks with him, she asked his secret.

'It's really quite simple,' the man explained. 'Twice each day, in the morning and in the evening, I expose myself in front of the tomatoes and they turn red with embarrassment.'

Desperate for the perfect garden, she tried his advice and proceeded to expose herself to her plants twice daily.

Two weeks passed and her buddy stopped by to check her progress.

'So', he asked, 'Any luck with your tomatoes?'

'No', she replied excitedly, 'but you should see the size of my cucumbers!'

A very shy guy goes into a bar and sees a beautiful woman sitting at one of the chairs, all on her own.

She is the most gorgeous woman he has ever seen and he simply can't keep his eyes off her.

After an hour of gathering up his courage he finally goes over to her and asks tentatively, 'Um, would you mind if I chatted with you for a while?'

She responds by yelling, at the top of her lungs, 'No, I won't sleep with you tonight!' Everyone in the bar is now staring at them.

Naturally, the guy is hopelessly and completely embarrassed. He slinks back to his table.

After a few minutes, the woman walks over to him and apologises.

She smiles at him and says, 'I'm sorry if I embarrassed you. You see, I'm a graduate student in psychology and I'm studying how people respond to embarrassing situations.'

To which he responds, at the top of his lungs, 'What do you mean, $200?'

Then there was the blonde working at reception at the big hotel. One of the bar workers comes up to her and says, 'Would you like to buy a raffle ticket? Janice in Housekeeping died suddenly last week. It's for her husband and four children.'

'No thanks,' the blonde receptionist says. 'I've already got a husband and two kids of my own.'

A man went to a strange town to be the guest speaker at a business meeting.

When he arrived at his hotel, he found he had a lot of time before the meeting, so he got the directions for a nearby golf course from the clerk.

While playing on the front nine, he thought over his impending speech and became confused as to where he was on the course.

Looking around, he saw a lady playing ahead of him. He walked up to her, explained the situation and asked her if she knew what hole he was playing.

She replied, 'I'm on the seventh hole and you are a hole behind me, so you must be on the sixth hole.'

He thanked her and went back to his golf.

On the back nine the same thing happened and he approached her again with the same request.

She said, 'Well, I'm on the fourteenth and you are a hole behind me, so you must be on the thirteenth.'

Once again he thanked her and returned to his play. He finished his round and went into the club house where he saw the lady sitting at the end of the bar.

He asked the bartender if he knew the lady. The bartender said that she was a sales lady and played the course often.

So the bloke approached her and said, 'Let me buy you a drink in appreciation for your help. I understand you are in the sales profession. I'm in sales also. What do you sell?'

She replied, 'If I told you, you would only laugh.'

'No I wouldn't.'

'Well if you must know,' she answered, 'I sell sanitary towels.'

And the bloke started laughing.

She said, 'See I knew you would laugh.'

'That's not what I'm laughing at,' he replied, 'I'm a toilet paper salesman, so I'm still a hole behind you!'

PUB FOOD AND DRINK

Two cheese and tomato sandwiches waltz into a pub. 'I'd like two beers, thanks,' asks one of them.

'Sorry, mate,' says the barman, 'We don't serve food here.'

Sadly, a peanut walked into a bar and was assaulted . . .

A skeleton walked into a bar and said, 'I'll have a Budweiser and a mop, please.'

A barman, who was rather stingy with dishing out the whisky, was giving a customer a drink.

As he handed the man his glass, the barman said it was extra good whisky, being twelve years old.

'Well, sir,' said the thirsty customer regarding his glass sorrowfully, 'It's very small for its age . . .'

IRISH

An Irishman is sitting at the end of a bar.
He sees a lamp at the end of the table.

He walks down to it and rubs it. Out pops a genie.

It says, 'I will give you three wishes.'

The man thinks a while. Finally he says, 'I want a beer that never is empty.'

With that, the genie makes a poof sound and on the bar is a bottle of beer.

The Irishman starts drinking it and right before it is gone, it starts to refill.

The genie asks about his next two wishes.

The man says, 'I want two more of these . . .'

Kelly limps into his favourite pub.
'My god! What happened to you?' the bartender asked Kelly as he hobbled in on a crutch, with one arm in a cast.

'I got in a tiff with O'Riley,' whispered Kelly to the bartender.

'O'Riley? He's just a wee fellow,' the barkeep said surprised. 'He must have had something in his hand.'

'That he did,' Kelly said. 'A shovel it was.'

'Dear Lord. Didn't you have anything in your hand?'

'Aye, that I did—Mrs. O'Riley's right tit.' Kelly said. 'A beautiful thing it was, but not much use in a fight!'

Two Irishmen, Murphy and O'Brien, grew up in the same village together.

They were friends all their lives, married a pair of sisters and lived just down the street from one another.

But now, Murphy had cancer and was lying on his deathbed, surrounded by his friends.

He calls, 'O'Brien, come 'ere O'Brien. I 'ave a request for ye."

O'Brien walks to his friend's bedside and kneels down.

'O'Brien, we've been friends all our lives and now I'm dying 'ere. I 'ave one last request fir ye to do.'

O'Brien bursts into tears, 'Anything Murphy, anything ye wish. It's done.'

'Well, under me bed is a box containing a bottle of the finest whiskey in all of Ireland. Bottled the year I was born it was. After I die and they plant me in the ground, I want you to pour that fine whiskey over me grave so it might soak into me bones and I'll be able to enjoy it for all eternity.'

O'Brien was overcome by the beauty and true Irish spirit of his friend's request.

'Aye, tis a fine thing you ask of me and I will pour the whiskey. But, might I strain it through me kidneys first?'

Three Englishmen were in a bar and spotted an Irishman. One guy said he was going to piss him off.

He walked over to the Irishman and tapped him on the shoulder. 'Hey, I hear your St Patrick was a sissy.'

'Oh really, hmm, I didn't know that,' replied the Irishman.

Puzzled, the Englishman walked back to his friends. 'I told him St Patrick was a sissy and he didn't care!'

The second Englishman said, 'You just don't know how to set him off, watch and learn.'

He walked over and tapped the Irishman on the shoulder. 'I hear your St Patrick was a transvestite!'

'Oh, wow, I didn't know that, thank you,' replied the Irishman.

Shocked beyond belief, the Englishman went back to his pals. 'You're right. He is unshakeable.'

The third Englishman said, 'No, no, no. I will really piss him off, you just watch.' The third Englishman walked over to the Irishman, tapped him on the shoulder and said, 'I hear your St Patrick was an Englishman.'

The Irishman responded, 'Yeah, that's what your friends were trying to tell me . . .'

Paddy and his two friends are talking at a bar. His first friend says, 'I think my wife is having an affair with the electrician.

'The other day I came home and found wire cutters under our bed and they weren't mine.'

His second friend says, 'I think my wife is having an affair with the plumber.

'The other day I found a wrench under the bed and it wasn't mine.'

Paddy says, 'I think my wife is having an affair with a horse.'

Both his friends look at him with utter disbelief.

'No I'm serious,' says Paddy.

'The other day I came home and found a jockey under our bed.'

Sister Mary Margaret enters O'Flynn's liquor shop.

'I'd like to buy a bottle of Irish whiskey,' she tells O'Flynn.

The owner of the store shakes his head and frowns. 'A bottle of Irish whiskey? And you being a nun too.'

'Oh no, no,' Sister Mary Margaret exclaims. 'It's for Father Reilly. His constipation, you know.'

O'Flynn smiles, nods and puts a bottle into a bag.

Sister Mary Margaret pays, takes the bag and goes on her way.

Later that day, O'Flynn closes shop for the day. On his way home he passes an alley. There in the alley is Sister Mary

Margaret. She's rip roaring drunk, the empty bottle at her side.

'Sister!' O'Flynn scolds.

'And you said it was for Father Reilly's constipation.'

'It is,' answers Sister Mary Margaret. 'When he sees me, he's gonna shit!'

Declan and Mick are knocking back a few pints of Guinness at the local when in walks O'Rourke.

He says, 'Did ye hear about O'Hara dyin' last night?'

Declan and Mick, in shock, exclaim, 'No! Poor O'Hara. Has anyone told his wife?'

O'Rourke says, 'No she hasn't been told yet, but I'll get sweet talking Patrick to tell her. He is such a sweet talker and so good with words that he can talk the fish out of the brook and the birds out of the trees.'

Just at the moment, in walks Patrick and says, 'Good mornin' to ye all lads, a pint on me for everyone.'

O'Rourke tells Patrick the sad news about O'Hara dying and asks him to break the news very gently to his wife, as she doesn't yet know. 'Seeing as you are the sweetest talker of us all,' adds O'Rourke.

Patrick, 'Well, I don't mind admittin' that I am and I will be glad to have a chat with O'Hara's wife and I'll break it so gently to her that a whimper is all she'll utter. I'm a man of words and I can charm the fish from the brook and the birds from the trees. Don't worry lads, I'll take care of this. They don't call me sweet talker for nothin'.'

Off they all go to O'Hara's house.

Patrick knocks on the door and O'Hara's wife answers and says, 'Yes may I help you?'

Sweet talking Patrick steps forward and at attention says, 'Are you the widow O'Hara?'

To which the woman responds, 'My name is O'Hara but I'm not a widow.'

Sweet talking Patrick braces himself and exclaims, 'Bullshit you ain't.'

Late one Friday night, a policeman spotted a man driving very erratically through the streets of Dublin.

They pulled the man over and asked him if he had been drinking that evening.

'Aye, so I have,' he said.

'It's Friday, you know, so me and the lads stopped by the pub where I had six or seven pints.

'And then there was something called "Happy Hour" and they served these drinks called margaritas, which are quite good. I had four or five of those, if my memory serves me well, which it usually does when it comes to matters of the drink. Then I had to drive me friend Mike home and of course I had to go in for a couple of glasses of the Guinness—couldn't be rude, you know. Then I stopped on the way home to get another bottle for later . . .'

The man dutifully fumbled around in his coat until he located his bottle of whiskey, which he held up for inspection.

The officer sighed and said, 'Sir, I'm afraid I'll need you to step out of the car and take a breath test.'

Indignantly, the man said, 'Why? Don't ye believe me?'

Father Murphy walks into a pub in Donegal and says to the first man he meets, 'Do you want to go to heaven?'

The man said, 'I do Father.'

The priest said, 'Then stand over there against the wall.'

Then the priest asked the second man, 'Do you want to get to heaven?'

'Certainly, Father,' was the man's reply.

'Then stand over there against the wall,' said the priest.

Then Father Murphy walked up to O'Toole and said, 'Do you want to go to heaven?'

O'Toole said, 'No, I don't Father.'

The priest said, 'I don't believe this. You mean to tell me that when you die you don't want to go to heaven?'

O'Toole replied, 'Oh, when I die, yes. I thought you were getting a group together to go right now.'

It seems that Pat, who was 88, had been feeling poorly for the past few months.

One day his son Seamus convinced him to go see the doctor.

After a complete exam, the doctor brought Pat and Seamus into his office. 'I've got bad news for Pat, your heart's near given out and you've only two months to live.'

Pat was stunned but after a few minutes he turns to his son and says, 'I've had a good long life and if the Lord wants me then I've no complaints.

'Let's be off to the pub, where I'm after having a pint with me friends.'

Arriving at the pub a few of his cronies spy Pat.

'Ah, Patty, how are you feeling today?' says one.

'Not good Mike, I've been to the doctors and he says I've two months to live.'

'What a shame,' says Mike, 'And what's ailing you?'

'The doctor says I have the AIDS.'

After a few moments Seamus gets his father alone and says, 'Da, it's not AIDS that you have, it's a heart condition.'

'Sure don't I know that, I just don't want them old buggers trying to sleep with your Ma when I'm gone.'

What are those two bulges at the front of your trousers?' asks the barmaid to the Irish customer.

'Ah, beejeezus,' says the bloke, 'Sure and they are hand grenades.

'You see, the next time that old queer, Gregory, tries to feel me up, I'll blow his bloody hands off . . .'

The priest was having a terrible time avoiding a nervous breakdown and had spent many a session on the blonde psychiatrist's couch.

As a last resort the good doctor ordered him to forget that he was a priest for a weekend, to go to the city, take the dog collar off, enjoy a few drinks and a bet at the casino and to live it up.

He did that and was having a wonderful time when he walked into a strip joint, sat down and ordered a stiff whisky.

'I'll get that for you straight away, Father,' said the hostess. The priest panicked.

'How do you know that I am a priest?' he stuttered.

'Oh, I'm Sister Mary, I go to the same psychiatrist as you do.'

PUB LOGIC

A bloke saunters into his local and sits at the bar. He orders three beers.

He takes a sip from one, then sips from the second, followed by a sip from the third.

He continues this way until each beer is polished off.

The same time the following week, the bloke comes in, sits at the same bar and orders three beers.

He takes a swig of the first, then the second then the third. He continues until they're gone.

The barman, curious about the behaviour, asks the bloke, 'Why don't you just order one beer at a time, mate?'

The bloke explains, 'I have two brothers. One lives in Seattle and the other in Sydney. The last time we got together we decided we'd start a ritual of having a beer together at this time every week.'

The barman thinks this is a lovely ritual and goes on about his business.

A week later the bloke's there again.

This time he orders only two beers. The curious barman tentatively enquires, 'Did something happen to one of your brothers?'

The bloke says, 'No, no. They're fine. I just decided I'd give up drinking.'

A drunk gets up from the bar and heads for the toilets. A few minutes later, a loud, blood-curdling scream is heard coming from the bathroom.

A minute passes and another scream from the bathroom fills the bar.

The bartender goes to the bathroom to investigate.

He yells, 'For God's sake, what's the bloody screaming about, you're scaring away my customers!'

The drunk responds, 'I'm just sitting here on the toilet and every time I try to flush, something comes up and squeezes the hell outta me balls.'

The bartender opens the door to check it out.

'You dickhead. You're sitting on the mop bucket!'

A guy walks into a bar. The bartender says, 'You've got a steering wheel down your pants.'

'Yeah, I know,' says the guy. 'It's driving me nuts!'

A man went into a bar and ordered a succession of Martinis.

After each one, he removed the olive and put it into a jar.

After two hours, the bartender felt compelled to ask, 'Why do you keep doing that?'

'Because,' slurred the man, 'My wife sent me out for a jar of olives.'

A man was sitting quietly at the bar when the bartender presented him with a riddle.

'My mother had a child. It wasn't my brother and it wasn't my sister. Who was it?'

The man thought for a minute but then gave up.

'It was me, you idiot!' exclaimed the bartender triumphantly.

The man thought it was a good trick and decided to play it on his wife when he got home.

He announced, 'My mother had a child. It wasn't my brother and it wasn't my sister. Who was it?'

His wife looked at him blankly and gave up.

He declared, 'It was Bazza at the Royal Hotel, you idiot!'

It was a dark, dark night and the drunk was making his way home after a rollicking evening at the pub.

He heard a faint cry for help off in the distance and full of good cheer, he followed the sound and came across a small wizard who had his foot caught under a large stone. He released the foot for the wizard and, as a token of his gratitude, the wizard granted him three wishes.

'I'll have a bottle of the best Scotch whisky,' said the drunk.

Sure enough there appeared a bottle of top shelf whisky and the drunk gulped it down.

'And what for your second wish?' asked the wizard.

'Make this a never ending bottle of the good stuff for me.' With a wave of his wand, his wish was granted.

'And for a third wish?' asked the wizard.

'I'll have another bottle like this,' slurred the drunk.

I SAY, I SAY

A dwarf walks into a bar and asks for a beer.
The barman says it'll cost him $3.50.
   The dwarf replies, 'Oh, umm. Can I give you $2.75? I'm a bit short . . .'

A man walks into a pub, goes up to the bar.
'Pint of your best,' he says to the barman.
   Whilst waiting for his drink he notices that Vincent Van Gogh is sitting at one of the tables.
   He goes up to him and says, 'Are you Vincent Van Gogh?'
   'Yes,' the old man replies.
   'Do you want a pint?'
   'No, ta. I've got one 'ere . . .'

A woman walked into a bar and asked for a double entendre, so the barman gave her one!

My dad was a great magician.
He was walking down the street the other day and turned into a bar.

A gentleman spots a nice looking girl in a bar, goes up and starts small talk. Seeing that she didn't back off he asked her name.
   'Carmen,' she replied.
   That's a nice name,' he said warming up the conversation, 'Who named you, your mother?'
   'No, I named myself', she answered.
   'Oh, that's interesting. Why Carmen?'

'Because I like cars and I like men,' she said looking directly into his eyes. 'So what's your name?' she asked.

'Beersex,' he replied.

Two guys are talking in a bar.
'My hobbies are hunting and drinking,' said one.
'What do you hunt?' asked the other.
'Something to drink.'

A moose walks into a bar and the barman says, 'Why the long face, buddy.'

The moose says, 'You'd have a long face too if you had sex only once a year!'

Q: How do you know that you are in a real lesbian bar?
A: Not even the pool table has balls.

A regular is chatting to her barman, 'Sometimes I wake up grumpy . . . other times I just let him sleep.'

An eel slides up to a bar and the barman says, 'Sorry, can't serve you.'

'Why not?' asks the eel.

'You're bloody legless.'

Barry was sick of waiting for his friend and was about to leave the pub when the friend finally turned up.

Barry said, 'Man, you should have been here 40 minutes ago.'

The friend replied, 'Why, what happened . . .?'

DRUNKS

Two drunks are staggering home one night and one decides to take a shortcut through the cemetery.

Halfway through an apparition appears.

'What's that on your back?' the ghost asks.

'It's a hump,' says the drunk.

The ghost puts his hand on the drunk's back and the hump disappears.

The drunk races home and next night at the pub he tells his mate all about it.

His mate is amazed and says he is going through the cemetery that night as he has a wooden leg and wants a proper leg.

Again, halfway through the cemetery a ghost appears. 'What's wrong with your leg?' he asks.

'It's a wooden leg,' says the drunk.

'Have you got a hump?' asks the ghost.

'No,' replies the drunk.

So the ghost puts his hand on the drunk's back and says, 'Here, you can have this one . . .'

A man walks into the front door of a bar. He is obviously drunk. He staggers up to the bar, seats himself on a stool and with a belch, asks the bartender for a drink.

The bartender politely informs the man that it appears that he has already had plenty to drink, that he could not be served additional liquor at this bar but could get a cab called for him.

The drunk is briefly surprised then softly scoffs, grumbles, climbs down off the bar stool and staggers out the front door.

A few minutes later, the same drunk stumbles in the side door of the bar.

He wobbles up to the bar and hollers for a drink.

The bartender comes over and still politely, but more firmly refuses service to the man, due to his inebriation.

Again, the bartender offers to call a cab for him.

The drunk looks at the bartender for a moment angrily, curses and shows himself out the side door, all the while grumbling and shaking his head.

A few minutes later, the same drunk bursts in through the back door of the bar.

He plops himself up on a bar stool, gathers his wits and belligerently orders a drink.

The bartender comes over and emphatically reminds the man that he is clearly drunk, will be served no drinks and either a cab or the police will be called immediately.

The surprised drunk looks at the bartender and in hopeless anguish, cries 'Man! How many bars do you work at?'

At 3 am, a receptionist at a hotel gets a call from a drunk guy asking what time the bar opens.

'It opens at noon,' answers the girl.

About an hour later she gets a call from the same guy, this time sounding even drunker.

'What time does the bar open?' he asks.

'Same time as before . . . noon,' replies the girl.

Another hour passes and he calls again, plastered. 'Whatime joo shay the bar opens at?'

The poor girl then answers, 'It opens at noon. You'll have to wait up until then before we let you in.'

'No . . . I don't wanna get in . . . I wanna bloody get OUT!'

A man is in a bar and falling off his stool every couple of minutes. He is obviously drunk.

So the bartender says to another man in the bar, 'Why don't you be a good Samaritan and take him home?'

The man takes the drunk out the door and to his car and he stumbles at least ten times. They drive along and the drunk points out his house to the man.

He stops the car and the drunk stumbles up the steps to his house with the man helping him out.

The drunk's wife greets them at the door. She says, 'Why, thank you for bringing him home for me, but where's his wheelchair?'

An absolute pisshead walked into a bar and, after staring for some time at the only woman seated at the bar, walked over to her and kissed her.

She jumped up and slapped him silly.

He immediately apologised and explained, 'I'm sorry. I thought you were my wife. You look exactly like her.'

'Why you worthless, insufferable, wretched, no good drunk!' she screamed.

'Funny,' he muttered, 'You even sound exactly like her.'

A drunken man is wandering around the parking lot of the pub. He is bumping into every car and rubbing his hand across the roof of each one.

The manager comes out of the bar and stops the guy.

'What the heck are you doing?' he asks the drunk.

'I'm looking for my car and I can't find it.'

'So how does feeling the roof help you?' he asks the drunk.

'Well,' the drunk replies, 'My car has two blue lights and a siren on the roof!'

A drunk rolled into a bar, but the bartender refused to serve him.

'I can tell from experience that you've had too much to drink,' he said. 'I'm not serving you.'

Five minutes later, the drunk came in again.

The bartender stood firm. 'There's no way I'm serving you more alcohol. You've had more than enough already.

Five minutes later, the doors opened and the drunk stumbled in again. 'Look,' said the bartender, 'I'm not serving you. You're too drunk.'

The drunk nodded. 'I guess I must be,' he said. 'The last two places said the same thing.'

ONE TOO MANY . . .

As a drunk guy staggers out of the bar one Friday evening, a fire engine races past, siren wailing and lights flashing.

Immediately, the drunk starts chasing the engine, running as fast as he can until eventually he collapses, gasping for breath.

In a last act of desperation he shouts after the fire engine, 'If that's the way you want it, you can keep your bloody ice creams!'

This big, nasty, sweaty woman wearing a sleeveless sundress walks into a bar.

She raises her right arm, revealing a big, hairy armpit as she points to all the people sitting at the bar and asks, 'What man out there will buy a lady a drink?'

The whole bar goes dead silent, as the patrons try to ignore her.

At the end of the bar, a skinny little drunk slams his hand on the bar and says, 'Bartender! I want to buy that ballerina a drink!'

The bartender pours the drink and the woman chugs it down.

After she's completed the drink, she turns again to the patrons and points around at all of them, again revealing her hairy armpit and saying, 'What man out there will buy a lady a drink?'

Once again, the little drunk slaps his hand down on the bar and says, 'Bartender! I'd like to buy the ballerina another drink!'

After serving the lady her second drink, the bartender approaches the little drunk and says, 'It's your business if you want to buy the lady a drink, but why do you call her a ballerina?'

The drunk replies, 'Sir! In my eyes, any woman who can lift her leg up that high has got to be a ballerina!'

A snake slithers into a bar and the bartender says, 'I'm sorry but I can't serve you.'

'Why not?' asks the snake.

The bartender says, 'Because you can't hold your licker.'

Three young lads went on their usual rounds around the pubs.

They came to one pub, got themselves a drink and after five minutes, an old drunken bloke in the corner staggers over to them and says, 'I've kissed your mum.'

One of the lads turns to the drunk and gives him the eye and turns back to his drink.

The drunk returns another five minutes later and shouts, 'Y'know what else buddy, I've been down on ya mum!'

The same lad turns around, frowns scornfully and returns to his drink with his friends. The old drunk returns yet again.

This time he says, 'I've been shaggin' your mum for the last 20 years.'

The lad in question stands up and says, 'Just go home dad! You're drunk.'

A man's been drinking in the bar alone for three hours straight and the bartender is getting worried about him.

He's downing whiskey sour after whiskey sour.

Finally, after the man orders his twelfth whiskey sour, the bartender shakes his head and says, 'Sir, I think you've had enough.'

The drunk looks at the bartender closely and says, 'Wha— what's that you shay?'

The bartender swallows.

'I said, I think you've had enough, sir.'

The drunk points a finger . . .

'Lis—l-l-listen Jack, I been drrrrrinking for shirty-thix years and I have no idea when I've had enough . . . so h-how the h-hell should y-y-you?'

A bloke goes into a pub, takes a seat at the bar and orders five pots.

The barman gives him an odd look since the bloke's all by himself, but he serves up the five pots and lines them up on the bar.

The bloke downs them . . . one, two, three, four, five.

He finishes the last one and calls to the barman, 'Four pots, please, mate!'

The barman serves up four pots and lines them up on the bar.

The bloke downs them . . . one, two, three, four.

Then he belches loudly, sways slightly on the stool and orders three more pots.

And one after the other, he knocks them back . . . one, two, three.

'Two potsh, mate!' he calls and the barman places two pots in front of him.

Down they go . . . one, two.

As the bloke slams the last one down on the bar, he says, 'One pot, mate.' So the barman fills the glass.

The bloke sits there, staring at it for a moment, trying to focus.

Then he looks at the barman and says, 'Y'know, it'sh a funny t'ing, but the less I drink, the drunker I get . . .'

One day, two drunks are in the toilets of a pub. One of them is bent over and the other has his finger up the other drunk's ass.

The bar manager comes in, sees the two of them and runs over to stop what they're doing.

'What the hell are you doing with your finger up his ass?' yells the bar manager.

'I'm trying to make him puke! He's had too much to drink, but you know how it goes, he wants to be sick, but he can't quite,' says the drunk.

'Well, you won't make him puke by sticking your finger up his ass,' the bar manager says.

'It will when I wave it under his nose . . .'

Two drunks are walking along the road in London. One turns to the other and slurs, 'Is this Wembley?'

'No, it's Thursday.'

'So am I! Let's go for a drink.'

Two old drunks were really lapping them up at a bar one night.

The first old drunk said, 'Yer know, when I was 30 and got a hard-on, I couldn't bend it with both hands. By the time I was 40, I could bend it about ten degrees if I tried really hard. By the time I was 50, I could bend it about 20 degrees, no problem. I'm gonna be 60 next week and now, bugger me, I can almost bend it in half with just one hand.'

'So,' says the second drunk, 'What's your point?'

'Well,' says the first, 'I'm just wondering how much stronger I'm gonna get!'

A bloke walks into a bar. 'Good evening, sir and what can I help you with this evening?'

'I'll have a scotch and a box of matches, please'

He then puts five cents on the bar and drinks the scotch.

'What's the five cents for?' asks the barman.

'That's for the matches. I didn't really want a drink, but you asked me so nicely that I felt obliged to drink it.'

'Sir I was only being polite. You have to pay.'

'I'm sorry, but I didn't really want the drink and I refuse to pay.' He is barred from the pub.

Two weeks later he walks back into the same bar.

The barman sees him and shouts, 'Out! We do not want you in here. I told you never to return again!'

The chap refuses and tells the barman that he must have mixed him up with somebody else as he has been out of the country and has only just returned that day.

The barman takes a closer look at him and says almost to himself, 'I don't understand it. You must have a double.'

'Thanks mate and I'll have a packet of matches as well.'

Two drunks were pulled up by the police.

'And what is your address?' the policeman asked of the first drunk.

'I'm Tom Smith and I have no fixed address.'

'And you?' said the cop, turning to the other drunk.

'My name is Peter Jones and I live in the flat above his . . .'

LEPRECHAUNS

Three leprechauns, Sean, Dennis and Kevin, are sitting in the pub getting quietly pissed when Dennis shouts out, 'Man, I'm bored wid bein' a tiny feckin' nobody. I'm tinkin' I'll take meself down to de Guinness Book of Records office and get meself entered in de book.'

'What de hell are ye talkin' about, ye eejit? You've dun nuttin' to get in de book for,' says Sean.

'Well, it's me hands, Sean,' Mick says, waving them around. 'I tink dey are de smallest in de world and I'm gonna get meself entered into de book and I'll be world famous.'

The other two agree that his hands are indeed quite small and they all carry on drinking heartily.

A little while later Kevin pipes up, 'Ya know Mick, if ye can get into de Guinness Book of Records for yer small hands, so can I.'

The other two smirk at each other and Mick says, 'How can ye have de smallest hands in the world if I've got dem, ya bloody fool?'

Kevin replies, 'It's not me hands, Mick, it's me feet.'

And he takes off his boots to show them.

'I tink dat dey are de smallest feet in de world and I'm gonna get meself entered into de Guinness Book of Records too.'

The other two agree that they are quite small and with that they all go back to their drinking.

Some time later Sean chimes in, 'Well, if youse two can get into de Guinness Book of Records, I can too.'

The others fall about laughing.

'What de feck have you got dat's so feckin' interesting?' cries Sean.

'It's me dick,' he says and pulls down his breeches to show

them. They both howl with laughter as Sean pulls out his little willy.

'Jaysus, ye've got the best chance of us all, Sean,' says Kevin.

'Dats the smallest feckin' dick I ever saw.'

And with that they all go back to their drinking.

Later on, full to the gills, they are heading home when, out of the corner of his eye, Mick spots the Guinness Book of Records office further down the street.

'Jaysus,' he says, 'I'm gonna go into dat office and I'm gonna get me hands measured.' And off he staggers.

Ten minutes later he comes out with a big smile on his face, waving his hands in the air. 'I did it. I did it,' he says.

'I'm in de Guinness Book of Records for de smallest hands in the world. Nobody's got smaller hands dan me,' he says.

And with that he pushes Kevin forward.

'Go on, ye eejit. See if ye have de smallest feet in de world. Go on.'

'Feck it. I will,' says Kevin and off he staggers.

Ten minutes later he too comes out with a big smile on his face, kicking his feet in the air.

'Jaysus, I'm famous,' he says. 'I've got de smallest feet in de world. I'm famous, I'm famous.'

With that Sean staggers to the office door. 'I'm gonna get me dick measured,' he says. 'I won't be long.'

The other two are waiting anxiously for Sean to return, but time slips by. Ten minutes turns into 20 and 20 into 30. No sign of Sean.

Forty minutes go by and the office door finally opens.

Sean slouches out looking disconsolate. 'Who de feckin' hell is John Howard?' he says.

An Irishman walks into a bar and asks for two beers. He then pulls a small green-skinned man out of his pocket and puts him on the counter.

As he's drinking one drink and the green man is drinking the other, an Englishman down the bar who has had a few too many drinks says, 'Hey, what's that little green thing down there?'

The green man runs down the bar, gives the Englishman a raspberry, SPLBLBLBLT! right in the face and runs back to the Irishman.

The Englishman mops himself off and says to the Irishman, 'Hey, what is that thing, anyway?'

The Irishman replies, 'Have some respect. He's a leprechaun.'

'Oh, all right,' the Englishman says sullenly.

They all go back to drinking beer.

An hour or so later, the Englishman is really plastered. 'Boy, that leprechaun is ugly!' he says.

The leprechaun runs down the bar and gives the Englishman a raspberry again—SPLBLBLBLBT!

This time the Englishman is really mad! 'Tell that leprechaun that if he does that again I'll cut his pecker off!' he shouts.

'You can't do that' says the Irishman. 'Leprechauns don't have peckers.'

'How do they pee, then?' asks the Englishman.

'They don't,' says the Irishman. 'They go SPLBLBLBLBLT.'

SURPRISE, SURPRISE

A sad looking, scrawny guy was sitting at a bar staring at his drink for ages.

Suddenly, a big biker came along, snatched his glass, guzzled down the contents and laughed, 'Hah! So what you gonna do about that, little man?'

'Oh, that'd be right,' sighed the little guy despondently.

'Today has been the worst day of my life. This morning I overslept and was late for an important meeting. My boss was furious and so he sacked me. I cleared my desk, went to my car, only to discover that it wasn't there—somebody had stolen it. So I got a taxi home, but when it came to paying the driver I realised I'd forgotten my wallet. I then had to go into my house, but I found my wife in bed with the gardener, so I left home and came to this bar and just when I was thinking about ending it all, you came along and drank my poison . . .'

Two drunken blokes stagger out of the pub and mistakenly stumble into a funeral parlour.

They bump about until one falls over the funeral piano.

'Here's a coffin,' he tells his mate.

'Do you recognise who's in there?' asked the other.

'No,' admitted the first drunk, 'But he sure had a good set of teeth.'

An infamous stud with a long list of conquests walked into his neighbourhood bar and ordered a drink. The bartender thought he looked worried and asked him if anything was wrong.

'I'm scared out of my mind,' the stud replied. 'Some pissed-off husband wrote to me and said he'd kill me if I didn't stop fucking his wife.'

'So stop,' the barkeep said.

'I can't,' the womaniser replied, taking a long swill. 'The prick didn't sign his name!'

OUTBACK PUBS

A little jackaroo goes into a pub. He yells over the crowd, 'Who the hell painted my horse yellow?'

A big burly bloke sculls his schooner, stands up and says, 'I did.'

The little jackaroo replies, 'Righto. Just wanted to let you know that the paint's dry.'

A bar owner in the outback has just hired a timid new bartender.

The owner of the establishment is giving his new hire some instructions on running the place.

He tells the timid man, 'If you ever hear that Big John is coming to town, drop everything and run for the hills! He's the meanest, biggest, nastiest outlaw who ever lived!'

A few weeks pass uneventfully. One afternoon, a local cowhand comes running through town yelling, 'Big John is coming to town! Run for your lives!'

When the bartender exits the saloon to start running, he's knocked to the ground by several townspeople scurrying out of town.

As he's picking himself up, he sees this absolute humungous, giant of a man approaching the saloon, probably about seven feet tall, muscular, grunting and growling as he walks.

He stomps up to the door, orders the poor barkeep inside and demands, 'I want a beer now!'

He pounds his heavy fist on the bar, nearly splitting it in half.

The bartender nervously hands the big man a beer, hands shaking.

The big bloke takes the beer, rips the top of the bottle off with his teeth and downs the beer in one gulp.

As the poor timid bartender cowers behind the bar, the big man gets up to leave.

'Do you want another beer?' the bartender calls out.

'Dang it, I don't have time!' the big man yells. 'I gotta get out of town. Didn't ya hear Big John is a-comin' . . .?'

A traveller walks into an outback pub. He can't help noticing two chunks of meat attached to the ceiling.

As he orders a beer he asks the barman, 'Hey, man, what's with the chunks of meat on the ceiling?'

'Well,' responds the barman, 'We've got a deal going. If you can jump up and grab the meat from the ceiling we'll shout your drinks all night. But,' he continues, 'If you can't get them down you shout the whole bar. Wanna give it a go?'

The traveller thinks for a minute and decides, 'Nah, sorry, the stakes are too high.'

A farmer walks into the Great Northern Hotel and finds the barmaid stalking flies with a fly swatter.

'Have you gotten any?' he asked.

The barmaid replied, 'Yeah. Three males and two females.'

'How can you tell the difference?' the farmer asked curiously.

'Three were on a beer can and two were on the phone!'

A jackaroo rode into town and stopped at the saloon for a drink.

Unfortunately, the locals always had a habit of picking on newcomers. When he left the bar some time later, he realised that his horse, who he loved dearly and which cost him a fortune, had been stolen.

The jackaroo rushed back into the bar, handily flipped his gun into the air, caught it above his head without even looking and then fired a shot into the ceiling. 'Who stole my horse!' he yelled with surprising forcefulness.

No one answered.

'I'm gonna have another beer and if my horse ain't back outside by the time I'm finished, I'm gonna do what I did up in Cairns. And let me tell you, I don't wanna have to do what I did up in Cairns!'

Some of the locals shifted restlessly.

The jackaroo had another beer, then walked outside to find his horse was back. So, he saddled up and prepared to ride out of town.

The bartender wandered out of the bar and said, 'Say cobber, what happened in Cairns anyway?'

The jackaroo turned back and said, 'I had to walk home!'

DOCTOR, DOCTOR!

A man collapsed on the floor of a pub, holding his belly and writhing in pain.

A barman quickly yelled, 'Is there a doctor in the house?'

A doctor came rushing up and knelt beside the sick man.

He felt a few places on his stomach and said, 'I can't be sure what's wrong with you, I think it's the drinking.'

'Okay,' the patient said. 'Maybe I should get an opinion from a sober doctor?'

A guy walks into a bar and approaches the barman, 'Can I have a pint of Less, please?'

'I'm sorry sir,' the barman replies, looking slightly puzzled, 'I've not come across that one before. Is it a spirit?'

'I've no idea,' replies the guy, 'The thing is, I went to see my doctor last week and he told me that I should drink Less.'

Three surgeons were at the pub and were arguing over who was the best surgeon in the land.

'One day,' the first one says, 'This guy came in with all his fingers in a bag of frozen peas. Without too many problems, I sewed them back onto his hands and he's now playing piano for the Queen of England!'

'Oh, that's nothing,' retorts the second one.

'One day this guy came in with his arms and legs cut off. With my skills, I sewed them back onto his body and now he's on the Olympic track and swimming teams!'

'Pff!,' snorts the third one.

'One day a guy high on cocaine was riding his horse when he was hit by a freight train. Unfortunately the bloke was decapitated and all that remained of the horse was it's ass. So I sewed the horse's ass to the body and now he is the Prime Minister of Great Britain!'

COP THAT

A man walks into a bar and within a few seconds the waiter goes running over to the man and says, 'Get out!'

'Why?' says the man.

'Well the other day you caused a lot of trouble in here and I'm not going to put up with that kind of behaviour.'

'I'm sorry,' says the man, 'But this is the first time I have been in here.'

'Well, then you must have a double,' replied the waiter sarcastically.

'Thanks a lot,' replies the man, 'Make it a whiskey.'

A bartender is taking out the bottles at the end of the night. On his return he notices a bloke sitting on the roof of the bar.

He stops, puzzled and asks, 'Excuse me mate, but what the hell are you doing up there?'

The bloke says, 'Because you bloody said drinks were on the house . . .'

A man in a bar has a couple of beers and the bartender tells him he owes $6.50.

'But I paid, don't you remember?' says the customer.

'Okay,' says the bartender, 'If you said you paid, you did.'

The man then goes outside and tells the first person he sees that the bartender can't keep track of whether his customers have paid.

The second man then rushes in, orders a beer and later pulls the same stunt.

The barkeeper replies, 'If you say you paid, I'll take your word for it.'

Soon the customer goes into the street, sees an old friend and tells him how to get free drinks.

The man hurries into the bar and begins to drink highballs when suddenly, the bartender leans over and says, 'You know, a funny thing happened in here tonight. Two men were drinking beer, neither paid and both claimed that they did. The next guy who tries that is going to get punched right on the face.'

'Don't bother me with your troubles,' the final patron responds. 'Just give me my change and I'll be on my way.'

A mundane looking fellow walked into a bar and sat down. After a few minutes, the bartender asked him if he wanted a drink and he said 'No thanks, I don't drink, I tried it once but I didn't like it!'

So the bartender said, 'Well would you like a cigarette?'

But the man said, 'No, I don't smoke, I tried it once but I didn't like it!'

The bartender asked him if he'd like to play a game of pool and again the man said, 'No I don't like pool, I tried it once but I didn't like it.'

'As a matter of fact I wouldn't be here at all, but I'm waiting on my son!'

The bartender said, 'Your only son I presume . . .!'

It's 40 below zero one winter night in Alaska. Pat is drinking at his local saloon and the bartender says to him, 'You owe me quite a bit on your tab.'

'Sorry,' says Pat, 'I'm flat broke this week.'

'That's okay,' says the bartender. 'I'll just write your name and the amount you owe me right here on the wall.'

'But,' says Pat, 'I don't want any of my friends to see that.'

'They won't,' says the bartender.

'I'll just hang your coat over it until it's paid . . .'

The other day, my friends and I went to a ladies nightclub. One of the girls wanted to impress the rest of us, so she pulled out a $10 note. When the male dancer came over to us, my friend licked the $10 note and stuck it to his butt cheek!

Not to be outdone, another friend pulled out a $20 note. She called the guy back over, licked the $20 note and stuck it on his other cheek!

In an attempt to impress the rest of us, my third girlfriend pulled out a $50 note! She then called the guy over, licked the bill and stuck it to his butt cheeks too.

Seeing the way things were going, the guy gyrates over to me.

Now everyone's attention is focused on me and the guy is trying to get me to top the $50.

My brain was churning as I reached for my wallet, 'What was I going to do?'

Then my habitual side took over, I got out my credit card, swiped it down the crack of his ass grabbed the $80 bucks and went home!

MARRIED

Q: What do the men in a singles bar have in common?
A: They're all married.

This guy leaves the bar, hoping he can get home early enough not to piss his wife off for drinking after work.

He gets home and finds his boss in bed with his wife. Later, back at the bar, the guy tells the bartender the story.

'Wow, that's awful, what did you do?' the bartender asked.

'Well, I carefully snuck back out the door and came straight back here.

'They we're just getting started, so I figure, I got time for a couple more beers.'

Larry was from the bush and went to the big smoke for the first time.

He got friendly with some of the local Melbourne lads and they took him to a classy bar.

'Amazin', just amazin', that's the city for ya,' he said, looking with delight into his glass.

'I've never bloody seen an ice cube with a hole in it!'

'I sure have,' said one of his new friends. 'Bin married to one for 15 years.'

Two married buddies are out drinking one night when one turns to the other and says, 'You know, I don't know what else to do. Whenever I go home after we've been out drinking, I turn the headlights off before I get to the driveway. I shut off the engine and coast into the garage. I take my shoes off before I go into the house, I sneak up the stairs, I get undressed in the bathroom. I ease into bed and my wife STILL wakes up and yells at me for staying out so late!'

His buddy looks at him and says, 'Well, you're obviously taking the wrong approach. I screech into the driveway, slam the door, storm up the steps, throw my shoes into the closet, jump into bed, rub my hands on my wife's butt and say, 'Let's do it!' And, she's always sound asleep.'

This guy walked into a bar with a monkey on a string. He sat at the bar and announced that the monkey is for sale.

The barman replied, 'I don't want any monkey! They destroy everything and they are a nuisance!'

The guy replied, 'But this is a special monkey. It gives a really good blowjob. Look, go in the back and try it out.'

After ten minutes, the barman returns with a broad grin.

'Man, that monkey is really good! I can't believe it. What a performance. How much do you want for it?'

On the spot, $200 was exchanged.

That evening, the barman returned home to his wife. 'Hi, dear. I just bought this monkey. I want you to teach it to cook and wash and then I want you to get the hell out of this house!'

A man was walking through a rather seedy section of town, when a bum walked up to him and asked the man for two dollars.

The man asked, 'Will you buy booze?'

The bum replied, 'No.'

Then the man asked, 'Will you gamble it away?'

The bum said, 'No.'

Then the man asked the bum, 'Will you come home with me so my wife can see what happens to a man who doesn't drink or gamble?'

LESSONS IN LIFE

WHY BEER IS BETTER THAN WOMEN

- You can enjoy a beer all month long.
- You don't have to wine and dine beer.
- Your beer will always wait patiently for you in the car while you play footy.
- When your beer goes flat, you toss it out.
- Hangovers go away.
- A beer label comes off without a fight.
- Beer is never late.
- Beer doesn't get jealous when you grab another beer.
- When you go to a bar, you know you can always pick up a beer.
- Beer never gets a headache.
- Beer stains wash out.
- After you've had a beer, the bottle is still worth five cents.

- A beer won't get upset if you come home and have another beer.
- If you pour a beer right, you'll always get good head.
- A beer always goes down easy.
- You can have more than one beer a night and not feel guilty.
- You can share a beer with your friends.
- You always know you're the first one to pop a beer.
- Beer is always wet.
- Beer doesn't demand equality.
- You can have a beer in public.
- A beer doesn't care when you come.
- A frigid beer is a good beer.
- You don't have to wash a beer before it tastes good.
- If you change beers you don't have to pay alimony.

THERE WERE THESE THREE FELLERS...

An Irishman, an Aussie and an American redneck were drinking in a neighbourhood bar.

After several hours, the topic of discussion turned to great bars they knew.

The Irishman said, 'There's this one bar back in Dublin called MacDougal's. At MacDougal's, if you buy two drinks, MacDougal, the man himself, buys you a third drink!'

The Aussie said, 'That's pretty good mate, but where I come from, there's a pub called Bazza's. At Bazza's, when you buy a drink, Bazza buys you a drink. You buy another drink, Bazza buys you another drink.'

The redneck finally spoke, 'You think that's good? Where I'm from, there's this place called Jack's. At Jack's, they buy you your first drink, they buy you your second drink, they buy you your third drink and then they take you out the back and get you laid!'

'Wow!' said the others. 'That's fantastic! That actually happened to you?'

'Well, no,' the man confessed, 'But it happened to my sister . . .'

An Irishman, an Englishman and a Scotsman go into a pub and each orders a pint of Guinness.

Just as the bartender hands them over, three flies buzz down and land in each of the pints.

The Englishman looks disgusted, pushes his pint away and demands another pint.

The Scotsman picks out the fly, shrugs and takes a long swallow.

The Irishman reaches into the glass, pinches the fly between his fingers and shakes him while yelling, 'Spit it out, yer bastard! Spit it out!'

An Englishman, an Asian and an Australian, attending a convention in a little town just outside Las Vegas, were standing in a seedy bar enjoying a few drinks.

The Englishman grabbed his wine glass, knocked it back in one gulp, then he threw the glass against the back wall, smashing it to pieces.

He told the other startled drinkers that the standard of living was so high in England that they never drank out of the same glass twice.

Next the Asian chap finished drinking his Margarita and threw his glass against the back wall.

He loudly proclaimed that in his home country there was so much sand and glass was so cheap that he too never drank out of the same glass twice.

Next the Australian drank his beer, drew a revolver and shot the Englishman and the Asian.

As he was returning the gun to his holster, he told the wide-eyed bartender that in Australia they had so many Englishman and Asians that they never had to drink with the same ones twice.

THERE WAS THIS YANK, SEE . . .

A Yank walks into a pub in Coober Pedy and lets rip with his voice to the crowd of drinkers.

He says, 'I hear you Aussies are a bunch of hard drinkers. I'll give 500 American dollars to anybody in here who can drink ten schooners of Coopers Stout back-to-back.'

The room is quiet. No one takes up the Yank's offer.

One man even leaves.

Thirty minutes later, the gentleman who left returns and taps the Yank on the shoulder.

'Is your bet still good?' asks the Aussie.

The Yank says yes and asks the bartender to line up ten schooners of Coopers Stout. Immediately the Aussie tears into all ten of the schooners, one after another then burps proudly.

The other pub patrons cheer as the Yank sits in amazement.

The Yank gives the Aussie the $500 and says, 'If ya don't mind me askin,' where did you go for those 30 minutes you were gone?'

The Aussie replies, 'Oh . . . I had to go to the pub down the street, to see if I could do it first.'

A Yank asks the Aussie barman why his American beer is served cold.

'So you can distinguish it from urine.'

A Yank buys an American beer for his Aussie friend.

'Hmmm,' says the Aussie as he takes a sip, 'That reminds me of being in my canoe.'

'Why's that,' asks the yank.

'It's fuckin' close to water.'

There are two men sitting in the pub and they are drinking their beers when one of the men looks to the end of the bar and realises that a bloke looking remarkably like Neil Armstrong, the first man to set foot on the moon, is sitting quietly at the end of the bar.

After some debate amongst themselves whether the man is Armstrong or not, one of the men gathers up the nerve to go up to the man and ask if indeed he is the American icon.

He gets to the end of the bar and asks, 'Excuse me sir, I couldn't help but notice that you look mighty like Neil Armstrong. Are you him?'

Mr Armstrong replies, 'Well yes I am. How may I help you?'

The man states that it was a pleasure to meet him since Neil Armstrong has always been a big idol and role model in his life.

Mr Armstrong thanks him and asks him what he does for a living. 'I am a journalist,' replies the man.

Mr Armstrong gives a sigh and replies 'Oh, okay.'

The man continues and asks him if he has a problem with journalists.

Mr Armstrong says no, but adds that reporters and the media had misquoted him many times on his moon walk statement.

The man asks him what he means and Armstrong replies, 'You guys reported I said "One small step for man, one giant step for man kind," but what I really said was "One small step for man, one giant step for Matt Kline".'

'Who the hell is Matt Kline?' says the man.

'Matt Kline has been a good friend of mine ever since we were kids,' replies Armstrong. 'We went to the same high school, the same college, we even served in the service at the same time. We where both in the Apollo space program but he didn't make the cut,' concluded Armstrong.

'Okay,' replied the man. 'So, it's just because you were great mates?'

'Well, there was one particular incident,' adds Armstrong.

'There came the day I was the best man at Matt's wedding and when the reception was over, I noticed that there were some packages left in the banquet room. Not wanting to have the couple go off without all of their gifts, I ran the packages up to their suite. When I got to the door I heard Matt's wife say to him, 'The day I put that in my mouth will be the day a man walks on the moon . . .!'

Two men from Texas were sitting at a bar, when a young lady nearby began to choke on a hamburger.

She gasped and gagged and one Texan turned to the other and said, 'That little gal is havin' a bad time. I'm a gonna go over there and help.'

He ran over to the young lady, held both sides of her head in his big, Texan hands and asked, 'Kin ya swaller?'

Gasping, she shook her head no.

He asked, 'Kin ya breathe?' Still gasping, she again shook her head no.

With that, he yanked up her skirt, pulled down her panties and licked her on the butt. The young woman was so shocked that she coughed up the piece of hamburger and began to breathe on her own.

The Texan sat back down with his friend and said, 'Ya know, it's sure amazin' how that hind-lick manoeuvre always works.'

THE GENIE

A bloke walks into a pub with an emu and a cat. They sit at the bar and the bloke orders three beers.

They finish their drinks and the emu shouts the next round.

They finish these and wait a moment, before the bloke orders the next three drinks.

The emu buys the next round; they drink them, wait a moment and the bloke buys three more.

Before they get up to leave, the barman can't contain his curiosity.

He leans over to the bloke and asks why the cat won't buy any of the drinks.

The bloke answers, 'Well, I found a bottle one day and I was granted one wish by the magic genie inside. So, I asked for a tall bird with a tight pussy.'

A guy walks into a bar, sits down next to another guy and immediately notices the guy has a very large Bic cigarette lighter.

The first guy says 'Wow, cool lighter . . . where did you get it?'

'A genie from this bottle granted me one wish.'

'Great, can I try it?'

'Sure.'

The first guy rubs the bottle and the genie appears. 'You are granted one wish,' says the genie.

The guy says, 'I want a million bucks!'

'Done,' says the genie and disappears.

A few minutes go by and suddenly the bar door swings open and thousands of ducks come pouring in.

Thousands and thousands of ducks falling all over each other through the bar door!

'I can't believe this,' says the guy who had just placed his wish, 'I asked for a million bucks, not a million ducks!'

The second guy then says, 'Do you really think I wished for a 12 inch Bic?'

A guy walks into a bar and sees a man sitting at the end with the smallest head he's ever seen. In fact, it is only about two inches high.

So, he sits down next to him and asks, 'How is that you have such a small head?'

The man replies, 'Well you see, I was stranded on a deserted island and was combing the beach, when I came across an ornate bottle. When I opened it to see what was inside, this beautiful genie with a fantastic body and beautiful face appeared and told me that I would be granted three wishes. My first wish was for a luxurious boat to take me home.'

'So,' says the new-found friend, 'did you get it?'

'Sure did,' the man continues, 'A large yacht appeared just off shore. Then for my second wish, I asked to be wealthy, so I would want for nothing when I got home.'

'And?'

The man goes on, 'A large pile of gold coins appeared on the deck of the yacht.'

'Wow! Then what happened?'

'I asked to make passionate love to the beautiful genie for

my third wish. The genie told me that under the rules, she
could not do that, so I asked, "How about a little head?"'

A guy walks into a bar with a cork shoved up his arse.
The bartender asks him how it happened so the guy sighs
and says, 'Well, I was walking along the beach when I came
across this magic lantern.

'I picked it up and started to brush off the dirt when all of a
sudden this genie pops out. The genie told me I could have
three wishes and I said, "No shit!"'

A HEALTH TIP

KEEP AWAY FROM BARS

The World Health Organization (WHO) has just issued an urgent warning about BARS (Beer and Alcohol Requirement Syndrome).

A newly identified problem has spread rapidly throughout the world.

The disease, identified as BARS (Beer and Alcohol Requirement Syndrome) affects people of many different ages.

Believed to have started in Ireland, the disease seems to affect people who congregate in pubs and taverns or who just congregate.

It is not known how the disease is transmitted, but approximately three billion people world-wide are affected, with thousands of new cases appearing every day.

Early symptoms of the disease include an uncontrollable urge at 6.00 pm to consume a beer or alcoholic beverage. This urge is most keenly felt on Fridays.

More advanced symptoms of the disease include talking loudly, singing off-key, aggression, heightened sexual attraction/confidence, uncalled-for laughter, uncontrollable dancing and unprovoked arguing.

In the final stages of the disease, victims are often cross-eyed and speak incoherently. Vomiting, loss of memory, loss of balance, loss of clothing and loss of virginity can also occur.

Sometimes death ensues, usually accompanied by the victim shouting, 'Hey Fred, bet you can't do this!' or 'Wanna see how fast it goes?' or 'Come on, you're all a pack of weak pricks.'

SEXY

A youngish chap goes into a pub and orders a shot of bourbon. He sculls it and orders another.

He sculls this one and orders again.

The barman quietly enquires, 'So, what's the occasion.'

The lad replies, 'My first blowjob.'

The barman smiles. 'In that case have a shot of top shelf, on the house.'

The lad drinks it and says, 'Now, if that can't wash the taste out nothin' will.'

A wombat walks into a pub orders a meal and starts chatting up a woman at the bar. After a while the woman explains that she's a prostitute and offers her services to the wombat.

They head upstairs and do the business.

As they return to the bar, the wombat says he needs to go to the toilet and that he will join her shortly in the bar for a drink.

After a while, the wombat does not return and the hooker becomes suspicious and starts to worry out loud about her payment.

The barman leans over at this point to explain, 'He won't be back. I'm afraid you've missed out with this character, lady. Y'see he's a wombat. All he does is eats roots and leaves.'

Morris starts talking to two women in a bar. They turn out to be Siamese twins and they wind up back at his apartment.

He makes love to one and then starts to work on the other.

Morris realises the first one might get bored watching, so he asks her what she'd like to do.

She says, 'Is that a trombone in the corner? I'd love to play your trombone.' So she plays it while he makes love to her sister.

A few weeks later, the girls are walking past Morris' apartment building.

One of the sisters says, 'Let's stop up and see that guy.'

The other sister says, 'Gee . . . I don't know . . . do you think he'll remember us?'

A man walked into a bar and as he walked in he saw a sign on the wall that said:

Cheese Sandwich, $3.00

Chicken Sandwich, $4.00

Hand Job, $10.00.

The man reached into his wallet and got out the proper amount of money. As he was doing so he saw this beautiful waitress and called her over. She walked up and said, 'Sir, can I help you?'

The man said, 'Why yes. Are you the one that does the hand jobs around here?'

She said, 'Why, yes I am,' with a sly grin.

The man looked up at her with a serious look, a slight grin, shaking his head and said, 'Well then darling . . . wash your hands and get me a cheese sandwich.'

These two buddies are sitting at the bar in a singles club and talking about another guy sitting at the other end of the bar.

'I don't get it,' complained the first guy, 'He's an ugly bastard, he has absolutely no taste in clothes and he drives a beat up wreck of a car, yet he always manages to go home with the most beautiful women here!'

'Yeah,' replies his buddy, 'He's not even very good conversationally, all he does is sit there and lick his eyebrows . . .'

Bert met Flo in a bar one night and began buying her drinks. They hit it off pretty well and soon Bert suggested they go to his apartment for some extracurricular activity.

Well, it wasn't long before they found themselves in bed making passionate love.

As they were making love though, Bert noticed that Flo's toes would curl up as he was thrusting in and out.

When they were done, Bert laid back on the bed and said, 'I must have been pretty good tonight. I noticed your toes curling up when I was going in and out.'

Flo looked at him and smiled. 'That usually happens when someone forgets to remove my pantyhose!'

Tom runs the bar and his wife Maude runs the bistro. One evening there's a hen's night in the bar. Tom gets very horny with all the gorgeous girls floating around.

He meets Maude upstairs and says, 'Come on, love, how 'bout a 69?'

Maude replies, 'What, Chicken Kiev at this time of night?'

Two guitars sit at a bar. One says to the other, 'C'mon babe. Let's go back to my place and get naked . . . no strings attached.'

DOGS

A man enters a bar with his dog. He takes a seat and orders a drink. The bartender says, 'You can't stay here with that dog.'

The man responds, 'But this is my seeing-eye dog.'

The barman apologises and offers a drink on the house.

Another bloke walks into the bar with a Chihuahua.

The first guy stops him and whispers, 'Look, mate, you won't be able to stay here unless you say that that's your seeing-eye dog.'

After thanking the guy for the tip he heads to the bar and orders a drink. The bartender says, 'Look mate, you can't stay in here with that dog.'

The guy responds, 'But this is my seeing-eye dog.'

The bartender says, 'Yeah right. They don't use Chihuahuas as seeing-eye dogs.'

To which the guy replies, 'What! They gave me a fuckin' Chihuahua?'

A man walks into a bar and sits down next to a lady with a dog at her feet. 'Does your dog bite?' he asks.

'No,' she says.

A few minutes later the dog attacks the man and bites his leg. 'I thought you said your dog doesn't bite!' the man shouts.

The lady says, 'That's not my dog.'

A Chihuahua, a Doberman and a Bulldog are in a bar having a drink when a hot little female Collie comes up to them and says, 'Whoever can say liver and cheese in a sentence can have me.'

So the Doberman says, 'I love liver and cheese.'
The Collie replies, 'That's not good enough.'
The Bulldog says, 'I hate liver and cheese in the morning.'
She says, 'That's not creative enough.'
Finally, the Chihuahua says, 'Liver alone . . . cheese mine.'

There are these three friends who get together to have a few drinks.

They talk about the night before when they decided to get drunk and find out who would do the stupidest stuff after they left the bar.

The first guys says, 'I was so drunk when I got home I stepped in the door and blew chunks.'

The second guy says, 'Well all I did was drive my new BMW into a telephone pole on the way home.'

The third guy says, 'You guys think that is bad? I went home, got into a huge fight with my wife, knocked over a candle and burnt the house down.'

All the guys chuckle for a bit. Then they try to decide who did the stupidest thing.

The first guy says, 'I don't think you guys understand. Chunks is my DOG!'

A guy walks into a bar and notices a big barrel filled with ten dollar notes.

He asks the bar tender, 'Why is that cooler filled with ten dollar bills?'

'Well, I tell anyone that if they want all of the money in the cooler that all they have to do is put $10 in the cooler and do three simple chores,' the bartender replied.

'Okay, what are the three things?' the guy asks.

'Well, first you must scull a bottle of whiskey.'

'Yeah, I'm up for that.'

'Second,' continues the barman, 'There is a rabid dingo out the back with a bad tooth. You've got to pull the tooth and bring it inside.'

'Okay, that's not too bad. What else?'

'There is a 90-year-old woman upstairs who has never had an orgasm. You've gotta go up there and give her one.'

The guy sits down and orders a drink and starts to think about the money. There had to be at least $10,000 in there and he was sure that he could do those three things.

After a few more drinks he decides to go for it.

'Okay, here's my $10. Give me that whiskey.'

So, the bartender puts the $10 in the cooler and hands him the bottle. Amazed, he watches as the guy finishes off the bottle.

Then, the bartender shows him the way to the door where the dog is. The guy stumbles outside the door and looks back at the bartender. The bartender then shuts the door and waits inside.

He listens and hears a lot of banging around. The bartender smiles as he pictures the hard time the guy must be having with the dog.

Suddenly, the guy comes stumbling back in, turns to the bartender and says, 'Now where's the old hag with the bad tooth?'

A guy comes walking into a bar with a turtle in his hand. The turtle's one eye is black and blue, two of his legs are bandaged and his whole shell is taped together with duct tape.

The bartender looks at the guy and asks, 'What's wrong with your turtle?'

'Not a thing,' the man responds, 'In fact, I'm willing to bet that this beat up turtle is faster than your dog!'

'Not a chance!' replies the barkeep.

'Okay then,' says the guy, 'You take your dog and let him stand at one end of the bar. Then go and stand at the other end of the room and call your dog. I'll bet you $500 that before your dog reaches you, my turtle will be there.'

So the bartender, thinking it's an easy $500, agrees.

The bartender goes to the other side of the bar and on the count of three calls his dog.

Suddenly the guy picks up his turtle and throws it across

the room, narrowly missing the bartender and smashing into the wall and says, 'I'll take it in hundreds, thanks!'

A blind man walks into a bar with a seeing-eye dog. When the blind man reaches the centre of the bar, he snatches the dog up by his collar and starts swinging him around and around.

The bartender speaks up and says, 'Hey what the hell are you doing?'

The blind man says, 'Just taking a look around.'

GOOD LORD!

Jesus walks into a pub and throws a few nails on the bar saying, 'Y'reckon you can put me up for the night?'

A drunk staggers out of a bar and spots two priests. He runs up to them and says, 'I'm Jesus Christ.'

The first priest says, 'No, son, I'm Jesus Christ.'

So the drunk says to the second priest, 'I'm Jesus Christ.'

The second priest replies, 'No, son, I'm Jesus Christ.'

The drunk says, 'Look, I can prove it,' and staggers back into the bar with the priests each side of him.

As soon as he walks in, the bartender takes one look at the drunk and exclaims, 'Jesus Christ, I thought we'd got rid of you!'

A man was sitting outside a bar enjoying a quiet drink, when a nun started lecturing him on the evils of alcohol. 'How do you know alcohol is evil?' said the man. 'Have you ever tasted it?'

'Of course not,' answered the nun. 'God forbid.'

'Then let me buy you a drink and, afterwards, if you still believe that it's evil, I promise I'll never touch another drop.'

'But I can't possibly be seen drinking,' said the nun.

'Right. Well, I'll get the bartender to put it in a teacup for you.'

The man went inside and asked for a beer and a vodka. 'And would you mind putting the vodka in a teacup?'

'Oh no,' said the bartender. 'Not that bloody nun again!'

The priest was having a heart-to-heart talk with a lapsed member of his flock, whose drinking of cheap cask wine invariably led to quarrelling with his neighbours and occasional shotgun blasts at some of them.

'Can't you see, Ben,' intoned the parson, 'That not one good thing comes out of this drinking?'

'Well, I sort of disagree there,' replied the drunk. 'It makes me miss the people I shoot at.'

SCIENCE

Two hydrogen atoms walk into a bar. One says, 'I think I've lost an electron.'
The other says 'Are you sure?'
The first says, 'Yes, I'm positive . . .'

A neutron walks into a bar. 'I'd like a beer,' he says.
The bartender promptly serves up a beer.
'How much will that be?' asks the neutron.
'For you?' replies the bartender, 'No charge.'

A barman was trying to convince one of his regulars the beer contains small traces of female hormones.
'It's true,' he said, 'The theory has been proven by scientists. They fed 100 men 12 pints of beer and observed that 100 per cent of them started talking nonsense and couldn't drive.'

Two builders go into the pub after a hard day's work.
They sit drinking for a while when a very smartly dressed man walks in and orders a drink.

The two began to speculate about what the man did for a living.

'I'll bet he's an accountant,' said the first builder.

'Looks more like a stockbroker to me,' argued the second.

They continued to debate the subject for a good while until eventually the first builder needed to use the toilet. On walking in, he saw the smartly dressed man standing at the urinal.

'Excuse me mate, but me and my friend have been arguing over what a smartly dressed fella like you does for a living?' the builder said to the man.

Smiling the man replied, 'I'm a logical scientist.'

'A what?' asked the builder.

'Let me explain' the man continued, 'Do you have a goldfish at home?'

A bit puzzled, but intrigued the builder decided to play along, 'Yes, I do as it happens.'

'Well then it's logical to assume that you either keep it in a bowl or a pond. Which is it?'

'A pond,' the builder replied.

'Well then it's logical to assume that you have a large garden.'

The builder nodded his agreement. So the man continued, 'Which means it's logical to assume you have a large house.'

'I have a six bedroom house that I built myself,' the builder said proudly.

Continued the scientist, 'Given that you have such a large house, it's logical to assume that you are married . . .'

The builder nodded again, 'Yes, I'm married and we have three children.'

'Then it's logical to assume that you have a healthy sex life.'

'Five nights a week!' the builder boasted.

The man smiled a little, 'Therefore it's logical to assume you don't masturbate often.'

'Never!' the builder exclaimed.

'Well there you have it,' the man explained, 'That's logical science at work. From finding out that you have a goldfish, I've discovered the size of your garden, all about your house, your family and your sex life!'

The builder left, very impressed by the man's talents.

On returning to the bar the other builder asked, 'I see that smart bloke was in there, did you find out what he does?'

'Yeah,' replied the first, 'He's a logical scientist.'

'A what?' the puzzled second builder asked.

'Let me explain,' the first builder continued, 'Do you have a goldfish at home?'

'No,' replied his mate.

'Well, you're a tosser then!'

WOOF, WOOF

A guy walks into a bar and sees a dog lying in the corner licking his balls. He turns to the bartender and says, 'Boy, I wish I could do that.'

The bartender replies, 'You'd better try patting him first.'

A highly timid little man ventured into a biker bar in a tough part of town and, clearing his throat, asked, 'Um, err, which of you gentlemen owns the Doberman tied outside to the parking meter?'

A giant of a man, wearing biker leathers, his body hair growing out through the seams, turned slowly on his stool, looked down at the quivering little man and said, 'It's my dog. Why?'

'Well,' squeaked the little man, obviously very nervous, 'I believe my dog just killed it, sir.'

'What?' roared the big man in disbelief. 'What in the hell kind of dog do you have?'

'Sir,' answered the little man, 'It's a four week old puppy Jack Russell.'

'Bullshit!' roared the biker, 'How could a tiny little puppy kill my big Doberman?'

'It appears that he choked on it, sir'

A guy walks into a bar with a small dog. The bartender says, 'Get out of here with that dog!'

The guy says, 'But this isn't just any dog . . . this dog can play the piano!'

The bartender replies, 'Well, if he can play that piano, you both can stay . . . and have a drink on the house!'

So the guy sits the dog on the piano stool and the dog starts playing—ragtime, Mozart and some Oscar Peterson numbers.

The bartender and patrons are enjoying the music.

Suddenly a bigger dog runs in, grabs the small dog by the scruff of the neck and drags him out.

The bartender asks the guy, 'What was that all about?'

The guy replies, 'Oh, that was his mother. She wanted him to be a doctor.'

A guy walks into a bar with his dog on a leash. The barman says, 'Geez, that's a weird dog: he's stumpy-legged, pink and doesn't have a tail. I bet my Rottweiler would beat the heck out of it.'

Fifty bucks is laid down. Out in the yard the Rottweiler gets mauled to pieces.

Another drinker says his Pit-bull will win and the bet is 100 bucks.

Another trip to the yard and when it's all over there are bits of Pit-bull terrier all over the place.

The drinker pays up and says, 'Say what breed is that anyway?'

The owner says, 'Until I cut his tail off and painted it pink it was the same breed as every other crocodile.'

THE POPE

Ascruffy old chap, reeking of booze, flopped on a barstool next to a priest.

The man's tie was stained, his face was plastered with red lipstick and a half empty bottle of gin was sticking out of his torn coat pocket.

He opened his newspaper and began reading.

After a few minutes, the dishevelled guy turned to the priest and asked, 'Say, father, what causes arthritis?'

'Mister, it's caused by loose living, being with cheap, wicked women, too much alcohol and a contempt for your fellow man.'

'Well I'll be,' the drunk muttered, returning to his paper.

The priest, thinking about what he had said, nudged the man and apologised. 'I'm very sorry. I didn't mean to come on so strong. How long did you have arthritis?'

'I don't have it father. I was just reading here that the Pope does.'

The general manager of Nescafe manages to arrange a meeting with the Pope at the Vatican.

After receiving the papal blessing, he whispers, 'Your eminence, we have an offer for you. Nescafe is prepared to donate $100 million to the church if you change the Lord's Prayer from "give us this day our daily bread" to "give us this day our daily coffee".'

The Pope responds, 'That is impossible. The prayer is the word of the Lord. It must not be changed.'

'Well,' says the Nescafe man, 'We anticipated your reluctance. For this reason, we will increase our offer to $300 million. All we require is that you change the Lord's Prayer

from "give us this day our daily bread" to "give us this day our daily coffee".'

Again, the Pope replies, 'That, my son, is impossible. For the prayer is the word of the Lord and it must not be changed.'

Finally, the Nescafe guy says, 'Your Holiness, we at Nescafe respect your adherence to your faith, but we do have one final offer. We will donate $500 million—that's half a billion dollars—to the great Catholic church if you would only change the Lord's Prayer from "give us this day our daily bread" to "give us this day our daily coffee." Please consider it,' says the manager and he leaves. The next day the Pope convenes the College of Cardinals.

'There is some good news,' he announces, 'And some bad news. The good news is that the Church will be coming into $500 million.'

'And the bad news, your Holiness?' asks a Cardinal.

'We're losing the Tip-Top Account . . .'

The Pope goes to visit the Seven Dwarfs who are drinking in a bar.

As he is finishing his speech on comparative religions, Dopey raises his hand to ask a question.

'Mr Pope, are there any dwarf nuns in Rome?'

'No Dopey,' responds the Pontiff, 'There are not.'

'Mr Pope, are there any dwarf nuns anywhere in Italy?' Dopey questions.

'No Dopey,' chuckles the Pope, 'There are no dwarf nuns in Italy.'

'Mr. Pope,' Dopey asks pleadingly, 'Are there any dwarf nuns anywhere in the world?'

'No Dopey,' the Pope says sadly, 'There are no dwarf nuns anywhere in the world.'

And softly in the background the six remaining dwarves start chanting, 'Dopey screwed a penguin, Dopey screwed a penguin.'

The Pope arrived in New York for a conference at a big hotel, but he was running a bit late. As he came out of the airline terminal he hailed a cab.

He said to the cabbie, 'I have to be at the hotel in ten minutes.'

'Ten minutes! It takes at least 40 minutes to get to that pub. I can't do it.'

'Well get out and let me drive,' said the Pope

The cabbie was a bit taken back by this, but it was the Pope so he jumped in the back while the Pope drove.

The Pope was flying along dodging in and out of traffic when he zoomed past a New York policeman.

The cop jumped on his motorbike and pursued the speeding vehicle. Finally when he caught up with it and pulled it over he asked the driver to wind down the window.

He then got on his radio for assistance.

'This is road patrol to base, I need some help.'

'What's up?' asked headquarters.

'Well I've pulled someone over for speeding and they are very important. What should I do?'

'How big are they—a local politician?' asked HQ.

'No, bigger than that.'

'The mayor of New York?'

'No, bigger than that.'

'A movie star?'

'No, bigger than that.'

'Not the President?'

'No, bigger than that.'

'Bigger than that?' asked HQ bewildered, 'Who the hell is it?'

'I don't know' replied the cop, 'But he's got the Pope driving him around.'

SPRUNG

Every night, after dinner, a man took off for the local tavern. He spent the whole evening there and arrived home very drunk around midnight each night.

He always had trouble getting his key into the keyhole and getting the door opened. His wife, waiting up for him, would go to the door and let him in.

Then she would proceed to yell and scream at him, for his constant nights out and coming home in a drunken state.

But, Walter continued his nightly routine.

One day, the wife was talking to a friend about her husband's behaviour and was particularly distraught by it all.

The friend listened to her and then said, 'Why don't you treat him a little differently, when he comes home? Instead of berating him, why don't you give him some loving words and welcome him home with a kiss? He then might change his ways.'

The wife thought that might be a good idea.

That night, Walter took off again, after dinner. And, about midnight, he arrived home, in his usual condition.

His wife heard him at the door and quickly went to it and opened the door and let Walter in.

This time, instead of berating him, as she had always done, she took his arm and led him into the living room.

She sat him down in an easy chair, put his feet up and took his shoes off.

Then she went behind him and started to cuddle him a little.

After a little while, she said to him, 'It's pretty late, dear. I think we had better go upstairs to bed, now, don't you think?'

At that, Walter replied, in his inebriated state, 'I guess we might as well. I'll be getting in trouble with the wife when I get home anyway!'

Awife was in bed with her lover when she heard her husband's key in the door.

'Stay where you are,' she said. 'He's so drunk he won't even notice you're in bed with me.'

Sure enough, the husband lurched into bed none the wiser, but a few minutes later, through a drunken haze, he saw six feet sticking out at the end of the bed.

He turned to his wife, 'Hey, there are six feet in this bed. There should only be four. What's going on?'

'Nonsense,' said the wife. 'You're so drunk you miscounted. Get out of bed and try again. You can see better from over there.'

The husband climbed out of bed and counted. 'One, two, three, four. You're right, you know.'

Abloke starts telling the barman his story, 'It was me birthday yesterday and I was expecting my wife to be pleasant and say "Happy Birthday" and probably have a present for me. She didn't even say "Good Morning," let alone any "Happy Birthday." I thought, well, that's wives for you. The children will remember. The children came down to breakfast and didn't say a word. When I started to the office I was feeling pretty low and despondent. As I walked into my office, my secretary, Janet said, "Good Morning, Boss, Happy Birthday." I felt a little better. Someone had remembered. I worked until noon, then Janet knocked on my door and said, "You know, it is such a beautiful day outside and it is your birthday, let's go to lunch, just you and me." I said, "By George, that's the greatest thing I've heard all day. Let's go." We went to lunch. We didn't go where we normally go. We went out into the country to a little private place. We had two martinis and enjoyed lunch tremendously. On the way back to the office, she said, "You know, it is such a beautiful day, we don't need to go back to the office, do we?" I said, "No, I guess not." She said, "Let's go to my apartment." After arriving at her apartment she said, "Boss, if you don't mind, I think I'll go into the bedroom and slip into something more comfortable." "Sure," I excitedly replied. She went into the bedroom and, in about six minutes, she came out carrying a big birthday cake, followed by my wife, children and dozens of our friends. They were all singing Happy Birthday. And there I sat on the couch, starkers with the biggest horn you have ever seen . . .!'

WOMEN

A poor man and woman sat down in their living room and the woman said, 'I'm going down to the pub for a bit, so put your coat on.'

The man replied, 'Oh, sweetie? Are you taking me with you?'

The woman replied, 'No, I'm turning the heat off.'

A young man walks into a singles bar with a roll of quarters taped inside the crotch of his jeans.

He looks around, then sits next to the most attractive woman there.

He was very pleased with himself after he noticed her constantly glancing down at his crotch.

'Hi, there, I'm Jerry,' he said, as he went into one of his well rehearsed routines, 'And I help produce a TV quiz show. Is there any question I can answer for you?'

'As a matter of fact there is,' she said as she glanced down once more toward his embellished jeans. 'Do you have change for a dollar?'

A guy walks up to a girl in a bar and asks, 'Do you want to play magic?'

'What's that?' she replies.

Grinning a little, he continues, 'You come back to my place, have sex, then disappear.'

A woman goes into a bar with a duck under her arm. Bartender says, 'What'll the pig have?'

The woman says, 'That's not a pig, that's a duck!'

'I know,' says the bartender, 'I was talking to the duck.'

A guy goes up to this girl in a bar and says, 'Would you like to dance?'

The girl says, 'I don't like this song, but even if I did, I wouldn't dance with you.'

The guy says, 'I'm sorry, you must have misunderstood me, I said you look fat in those pants.'

This guy has been sitting in a bar all night, staring at a girl wearing the tightest pants he's ever seen. Finally his curiosity gets the best of him.

So he walks over and asks, 'How do you get into those pants?'

The young woman looks him over and replies, 'Well, you could start by buying me a drink . . .'

A woman in the bar says that she wants to have plastic surgery to enlarge her breasts. A bar fly tells her, 'Hey, you don't need surgery to do that. I know how to do it without surgery.'

The lady asks, 'How do I do it without surgery?'

'Just rub toilet paper between them.'

Startled the lady asks, 'How does that make them bigger?'

'I don't know, but it worked for your ass.'

A man meets a gorgeous woman in a bar. They talk, they connect, they end up leaving together.

They get back to her place and as she shows him around her apartment, he notices that her bedroom is completely packed with teddy bears.

Hundreds of small bears on a shelf all the way along the floor, medium sized ones on a shelf a little higher and huge bears on the top shelf along the wall.

The man is kind of surprised that this woman would have a collection of teddy bears, especially one that's so extensive, but he decides not to mention this to her.

After a night of passion, as they are lying together in the afterglow, the man rolls over and asks, smiling, 'Well, how was it?'

She replied, 'You may select any prize from the bottom shelf.'

There is a woman sitting with a bunch of guys at a bar. The guys were all showing off their tattoos and uttering sexist remarks as to how women cannot take enough pain to get a tattoo.

After listening to the guys gloat for a little bit longer, the woman states, 'Well, I have a tattoo, too!'

The men all look surprised.

The woman continues, 'I have a tattoo of a cute little grey mouse in a rather private place. Do you want to see my tattoo?'

The guys are getting excited as the crowd starts gathering around the woman.

Without much ado, the woman stands up, undoes her pants and drops them. She then looks down, looks kind of confused and gives the men a wimpy smile.

One of the men asks, 'What's wrong, sweet lady?'

The woman, with a big smile on her face, answers, 'Oh, nothing, I can't show you my little mouse tattoo after all. My pussy must have eaten it.'

A sleazebag slides up beside a woman at a bar and says, 'Is there a mirror in your pocket? Because I can definitely see myself in your pants tonight.'

A woman walks into a bar with a duck on her head. The bartender says, 'May I help you, sir?'

The duck says, 'Yeah. Help me get this human out of my ass.'

INJURIES

A regular at Ralphy's tavern came in one evening sporting a matched pair of swollen black eyes that appeared extremely painful.

'Whoa, Sam!' said the bartender. 'Who gave those beauties to you?'

'Nobody gave them to me,' said Sam. 'I had to fight like crazy for both of them.'

Two gas company servicemen, a senior training supervisor and a young trainee, were out checking meters at a local pub.

They parked their truck at the end of the alley and walked to the other end.

A woman who was sitting in the bar having a lemon, lime and bitters watched the two men as they checked the gas meter.

Finishing the meter check, the senior supervisor challenged his younger co-worker to a foot race down the alley back to the truck to prove that an older guy could outrun a younger one.

As they came running up to the truck, they realised the lady from the bar was huffing and puffing right behind them.

They stopped and asked her what was wrong.

Gasping for breath, she replied, 'When I see two gas men running as hard as you two were, I figured I'd better run too . . .!'

Harry was playing off the sixth tee at the local golf course. The fairway of the sixth needed some skill because it ran alongside the road.

But Harry sliced the ball badly and it disappeared over the hedge bordering the road.

So he put another ball down and took the penalty.

A few days later, he was having a quiet beer in the pub, when the golf pro rushes in.

'Excuse me Harry, but was it you who sliced this ball into the road at the sixth on Tuesday morning?' said the pro.

'Yes, but I took the penalty.'

'That's as may be. But you might be interested to know that your ball hit and killed a small boy on a tricycle, the tricycle fell in the path of a Mountie on a motorcycle. He skidded and was thrown through the window of a car, killing the nun at the wheel. The car then swerved into a cement mixer which wasn't too damaged but had to veer slightly and in doing so ran into the local school bus with such an impact that it sent it flying through the window of the shopping centre. At last count from the hospital there are 13 people dead and 79 people seriously injured.'

The golfer turned a deathly shade of white and said, 'What can I do?'

'Well, you could try moving your left hand a little bit further down the shaft,' the pro advised . . .

SPORT

A golf club walks into a local bar and asks the barman for a pint of beer.

The barman refuses to serve him. 'Why not?' asks the golf club.

'You'll be driving later,' replies the bartender.

O ne day, John visits the big city, comes out of the pub and sitting by the door is an American Indian gentleman with full head gear on, sitting cross legged on the pavement with a sign written on the back of a beer carton which said, 'Marvo the Marvellous Memory Man'/Give me a dollar, ask me a question/If I am unable to answer it, I shall give you $10.'

'Hello!' said John.

'Where I come from it is polite to say, "HOW?"' said the Indian.

'Sorry,' said John. So he went out and tried again.

"HOW?" he greeted the Indian. He gave him a dollar and then asked, 'Who won the Scottish FA Cup in 1945?'

The Indian thought for a bit and gave his answer.

'Rangers beat Kilmarnock 4-1.'

John was amazed.

Ten years passed.

John is in the same city again and walking down the same street and recognises the pub.

This time he sees a massive building next to it, with a sign written in neon lights 'MARVO THE MEMORY MAN.'

John walks in and sees the same man sitting at a table.

Remembering his manners, John looks at the little man and says "HOW?"

The man looks at him and says, 'Great Cross, bullet header, top left hand corner.'

An Englishman, an Australian and an Arab are sitting in a bar. The Englishman says, 'I've got ten children, one more and I'll have a soccer team.'

The Australian man says, 'I've got 14 children, one more and I'll have a rugby team.'

The Arab says, 'I've got 17 wives, one more and I'll have a golf course.'

David Beckham was in the hotel lobby and spied a soft drink machine. He goes up and puts in a dollar and out rolls a tin of Coca Cola.

So he puts in another dollar.

This time a can of Fanta rolls out, so he puts in another dollar.

By this time a queue has formed waiting to get a drink and the impatient Yank next in line says, 'Come on buddy, give us a break. Get a move on. We're waiting.'

To which our football hero replies, 'Bugger off, man, I'm winning!'

Stevie Wonder and Tiger Woods are having a quiet beer in a dingy pub, away from the adoring fans.

Tiger turns to Stevie and says: 'How is the singing career going?'

Stevie Wonder says,: 'Not too bad, the latest album has gone into the top 10, so all in all I think it is pretty good.

'So, how about you? How is the golf?'

Tiger replies, 'Not too bad, I am not winning as much as I used to but I'm still making a bit of money.

'I have some problems with my swing. But I think I have got that right now.'

Stevie Wonder says, 'I always find that when my swing goes wrong, I need to stop playing for a while and think about it, then the next time I play it seems to be all right.'

Tiger says, 'You play golf!'

Stevie says, 'Yes, I have been playing for years.'

And Tiger says, 'But I thought you were blind, how can you play golf if you are blind?'

Stevie replies, 'I get my caddie to stand in the middle of the fairway and he calls to me, I listen for the sound of his voice and play the ball towards him, then when I get to where the ball lands the caddie moves to the green or further down the fairway and again I play the ball towards his voice.'

'But how do you putt?'

'Well,' says Stevie, 'I get my caddie to lean down in front of the hole and call to me with his head on the ground and I just play the ball to the sound of his voice.'

Tiger says, 'What is your handicap?'

Stevie says, 'Well, I play off scratch.'

Tiger is incredulous and says to Stevie, 'We must play a game sometime.'

Wonder replies, 'Well, people don't take me seriously, so I only play for money and I never play for less than $100,000 a hole.'

Tiger thinks it over and after concluding that his career is on the slide and a few hundred grand wouldn't go astray, says, 'Okay, I'm up for that—when would you like to play?'

Stevie Wonder replies, 'I don't care, any night next week is okay with me.'

After an enjoyable 18 holes of golf, a man stopped in a bar for a beer before heading home.

There he struck up a conversation with a ravishing young beauty.

They had a couple of drinks, liked each other and soon she invited him over to her apartment.

For two hours they made mad, passionate love.

On the way home, the man's conscience started bothering him something awful. He loved his wife and didn't want this unplanned indiscretion to ruin their relationship, so he decided the only thing to do was come clean.

'Honey,' he said when he got home, 'I have a confession to make. After I played golf today, I stopped by the bar for a beer, met a beautiful woman, went back to her apartment and made mad passionate love to her for two hours. I'm sorry, it won't ever happen again and I hope you'll forgive me.'

His wife scowled at him and said, 'Don't lie to me, you sorry scumbag! You played 36 holes, didn't you?'

This blokes walks into one of those classy sports club bars with a monkey on his shoulders.

He takes a seat at the bar, lets the monkey go and orders a drink.

The monkey is running wild through the bar, swinging from the lights, jumping on the tables and showing off.

The monkey then jumps up on a display of sporting memorabilia, throwing stuff all over the place.

Out of all the stuff—footballs, trophies, cricket bats, award winning medals and so on, he grabs a golf ball, once used by Greg Norman to win the British Open and swallows it.

By now, the bartender is really annoyed.

The gentleman who owns the monkey apologises, pays for his drink and the ball then leaves with his monkey.

A couple of weeks later the man returns with his monkey.

He sits at the bar and lets the monkey run wild again.

He jumps up on the bar where he spies a bowl of grapes.

He grabs a grape and shoves it up his ass, pulls it out and then eats it.

The bartender is totally grossed out.

'Did you see what your monkey just did?' he asks the man.

The man replies, 'Oh yeah, since that golf ball incident, he measures everything!'

DISTRESSING TIMES

Harold ambles into his local to meet his friend. As he approaches, the friend comments, 'You look terrible. What's the problem?'

'My mother died in August,' Harold said, 'And left me $25,000.'

'Gee, that's tough,' he replied.

'Then in September,' Harold continued, 'My father died, leaving me $90,000.'

'Wow. Two parents gone in two months. No wonder you're depressed.'

'And last month my aunt died and left me $15,000.'

'Three close family members lost in three months? How sad.'

'Then this month,' continued, Harold, 'Not a bloody cent from no-one!'

Brenda O'Malley is home making dinner as usual, when Tim Finnegan arrives at her door. 'Brenda, may I come in?' he asks. 'I've somethin' to tell ya.'

'Of course you can come in. You're always welcome, Tim. But where's my husband?'

'That's what I'm here to be tellin' ya, Brenda. There was an accident down at the Guinness brewery.'

'Oh, God no!' cries Brenda. 'Please don't tell me . . .'

'I must, Brenda. Your husband Seamus is dead and gone. I'm sorry.'

Finally, she looked up at Tim. 'How did it happen, Tim?'

'It was terrible, Brenda. He fell into a vat of Guinness Stout and drowned.'

'Oh my dear Jesus! But you must tell me true, Tim. Did he at least go quickly?'

'Well, no Brenda, no.'

'No?'

'Fact is, he got out three times to pee.'

A bloke went into a bar and ordered six double vodkas. Fred, the bartender said, 'Wow, you must have had a bad day.'

'Yeah', said the bloke, 'I just found out my older brother is gay.'

The next day the bloke showed up and again ordered six doubles.

Fred said, 'What, more problems.'

And the bloke replied, 'Damn right, I just found out that my younger brother is gay.'

The third day, the same routine—six doubles.

Fred said, 'What the hell! Doesn't anyone in your family like women?'

'Yeah', said the bloke, 'I just found out my wife does . . .'

WELL, I'LL BE . . .

A man stumbles up to the only other patron in a bar and asks if he could buy him a drink. 'Why of course,' comes the reply.

The first man then asks, 'Where are you from?'

'I'm from Tasmania,' replies the second man.

The first man responds, 'You don't say, I'm from Tassie too! Let's have another round to Tasmanians.'

'Of course,' replies the second man.

'I'm curious', the first man then asks, 'Where in Tassie are you from?'

'Devonport,' comes the reply.

'I can't believe it,' says the first man. 'I'm from Devonport too! Let's have another drink to good old Devo.'

'Of course,' replies the second man.

Curiosity again strikes and the first man asks, 'What school did you go to?'

'Saint Mary's,' replies the second man, 'I graduated in '62.'

'This is unbelievable!' the first man says. 'I went to Saint Mary's and I graduated in '62, too!'

About that time, in comes one of the regulars and sits down at the bar. 'What's been going on?' he asks the bartender.

'Nothing much,' replies the bartender. 'The Faraday twins are drunk again.'

I walked into a bar the other day and ordered a double. The bartender brought out a guy who looked just like me.

A proud new father from Wagga Wagga buys a round of drinks for everyone in the bar and announces that his wife has just produced a typical Wagga baby boy, weighing a whopping 20 pounds.

'Wow!' everyone cheers, amazed at the size of the baby.

A week later the father returns to the bar. The bartender asks, 'How much does your baby boy weigh now?'

The proud father answers, 'A whopping 10 pounds!'

The bartender says, 'What? I know that babies lose a little weight after birth, but ten pounds? How did he lose 10 pounds in one week?'

The proud father says, 'I had him circumcised!'

TRY ONE MORE TIME?

A big burly logger walks into the Cricketers Arms. He's a rather scary looking guy. He orders a beer, sculls it and bellows, 'All you guys on this side of the bar are a bunch of idiots!' A sudden silence descends.

After a moment he asks, 'Anyone got a problem with that?' The silence lengthens.

He then chugs back another beer and growls, 'And all you guys on the other side of the bar are all scum!' Once again, the bar is silent.

He looks around belligerently and roars, 'Anyone got a problem with that?' A lone man gets up from his stool unsteadily and starts to walk towards the man.

'You got a problem, buddy?'

'Oh no, I'm just on the wrong side of the bar.'

Two Swedish guys get off a ship and head for the nearest bar at the pier.

Each one orders two whiskeys and immediately downs them. They then order two more whiskeys apiece and quickly throw them back. They then order another two whiskeys apiece.

One of the men picks up one of his drinks and turning to the other man, says, 'Skol!'

The other man turns to the first and says, 'Hey, did you come here to bullshit or did you come here to drink?'

A man had been drinking at the bar for hours when he mentioned something about his girlfriend being out in the car.

The bartender, concerned because it was so cold, went to check on her.

When he looked inside the car, he saw the man's buddy, Pete and his girlfriend going at it in the backseat.

The bartender shook his head and walked back inside.

He told the drunk that he thought it might be a good idea to check on his girlfriend. The fellow staggered outside to the car, saw his buddy and his girlfriend entwined, then walked back into the bar laughing.

'What's so funny?' the bartender asked. 'That stupid Pete!' the fellow chortled, 'He's so drunk, he thinks he's me!'

A guy walks into a bar carrying a very talented octopus. He says as much to the patrons of the bar and bets $500 that the octopus can play any musical instrument that the guys can produce.

One guy accepts. He lays $500 on the bar, says, 'Here's $500 that he can't play my trumpet.'

So he goes home and gets his trumpet. The octopus looks at it, scratches its head, turns it over, then starts to play, the most beautiful sound anyone has ever heard from a trumpet.

The owner pockets his new $500.

Another guy says 'Here's $500 that he can't play my clarinet.'

So he produces the instrument and the octopus looks at it, turns it over, then starts to play, the most beautiful sound anyone has ever heard from a clarinet.

The owner pockets his $500.

Another guy says, 'Here's $500 that he can't play my bagpipes.'

So he gets his pipes and the octopus looks at them, puzzled, then looks at them some more.

He does so for about five minutes, then throws the instrument across the room and starts cussing.

The challenger takes his $500 and his pipes and leaves.

The owner of the octopus is furious. He says to the creature, 'What the hell was that? You just cost me $500, you know.'

The octopus shrugs and says, 'Well. I was gonna shag it, but I couldn't get its pyjamas off.'

RUGBY

He was on the way to Wimbledon one Saturday, when he stepped into a pub just near Southfields tube station to watch the rugby.

He considered himself a patriotic Australian, but watching rugby in England amongst a sea of red, it was sometimes better to be diplomatically silent.

However, a group of Aussies had already camped themselves in a corner and were gearing up for a bit of banter.

A conversation between two Aussies followed, one of them obviously Victorian and an Aussie Rules fan, as he didn't know anything about rugby.

'The team is made up of the best players from Ireland, England, Wales and Scotland,' his mate told him.

'So it's an All Star team then?'

'Not really.'

'But four countries, five countries if you count Northern Ireland as a separate country, against one. Is that fair?'

His mate looked around for help.

Our friend told him about the tradition of the Lions and the enormous interest they create.

As the game progressed and the Aussie corner became more and more invisible, the Victorian spoke up again.

'If they're so good, how did we become the world champions?'

'They can't play in the World Cup,' came the reply.

'So, in the scheme of things, this means absolutely nothing.'

His mate looked like the straight man in a comedy duo. As the English became more and more rowdy, the Victorian became more and more patriotic.

One Englishman threw a comment his way, 'You're getting killed, you dirty Aussie bastards!'

The Victorian launched into him.

'Five countries versus one. A country of 20 million, where only two states play the game. Even those two states divide the best players into rugby league and rugby union. What the hell are you proud of?'

A SERIOUS WARNING

Our Government just can't help it. They must try to regulate and control everything. Now they are seriously considering warning us against the demon drink by putting warnings on the labels of our alcoholic beverages. So let's be practical and tell it how it is.

Warning: Consumption of alcohol may make you think you are whispering when you are actually shouting loudly.

Warning: Consumption of alcohol may create the illusion that you are tougher, more handsome, smarter, talk better and fight harder than a really, really, really big biker named 'Killer McKenzie'.

Warning: Consumption of alcohol may cause obstruct the time-space continuum. Small and sometimes large, gaps of time may disappear from your memory bank.

Warning: Consumption of alcohol may cause you to tell the Managing Director what you really think about him and his crappy little company while photocopying your bum at the staff Christmas Party.

Warning: Consumption of alcohol can make you dance like a jerk.

Warning: Consumption of alcohol may lead you to believe that ex-girlfriends are really dying for you to telephone them at four o'clock in the morning.

Warning: Consumption of alcohol may cause you to tell the same indescribably boring story over and over again.

Warning: Consumption of alcohol may cause you to thay things like thish.

Warning: Consumption of alcohol may leave you wondering what the hell ever happened to your pants anyway.

Warning: Consumption of alcohol may cause you to roll over in the morning and see something really scary.

Warning: Consumption of alcohol is the leading cause of inexplicable rug burn on the forehead.

Warning: Consumption of alcohol may lead you to believe you are invisible.

Warning: Consumption of alcohol may lead you to think people are laughing with you.

YOU DON'T SAY?

This guy walks into a bar and sits down next to a good-looking woman and starts looking at his watch. The woman notices this and asks him if his date is late.

'No,' he replies. 'I've just got this new state-of-the-art watch and I was just about to test it.'

'What does it do?'

'It uses alpha waves to telepathically talk to me.'

'What's it telling you now?'

'Well, it says you're not wearing a bra or panties.'

'Ha! Well it must be broken then, because I am!'

'Darn thing must be an hour fast.'

A young nerd at a pub sculls three pints in a row. The barman, knowing that the nerd is not usually a drinker, asks what's up.

'I'm preparing for a test,' replies the nerd.

The barman says, 'Well, I don't think drinking all that beer's gonna help you much.'

'Oh, it should,' replies the nerd, 'It's a urine test.'

Three mice were sitting at a bar talking about how tough they were. The first mouse slams a shot and says, 'I play with mouse traps for fun. I'll run into one on purpose and as it is closing on me, I grab the bar and bench press it 20 to 30 times.' And, with that, he slams another shot.

The second mouse slams a shot and says, 'That's nothing. I take those poison bait tablets, cut them up and snort them, just for the fun of it.' And, with that, he slams another shot. The third mouse slams a shot, gets up and walks away.

The first two mice look at each other, then turn to the third mouse and ask, 'Where the hell are you going?'

The third mouse stops and replies, 'I'm going home to shag the cat.'

Q. What's the difference between the ugly door bitch at your local pub and a supermodel?
A. About 12 beers.

One telephone slides up to another at the bar and smoothly suggests, 'C'mon babe . . . how 'bout it.'
'Sorry,' says the other phone, 'I'm engaged.'

HOW TO TELL

CHARACTER INDICATORS AT THE PUB URINAL

This will give you a guide to the background of the man standing next to you next time you are having a leak at the pub:

Sociable: Joins friends in pissing whether he has to go or not.

Crosseyed: Looks into next urinal to see how the other guy is fixed.

Timid: Cannot piss if someone is watching, flushes urinal and comes back later.

Indifferent: All urinals being in use, he pisses in the sink.

Worried Not sure of where he has been lately, makes a quick inspection.

Frivolous: Plays stream up, down and across urinals, tries to hit fly or bug.

Absent-minded: Opens vest, pulls out his tie, pisses in his pants.

Childish: Pisses directly in bottom of urinal, likes to see it bubble.

Sneak: Farts silently while pissing, acts very innocent, knows the man in the next stall will get blamed.

Tough: Bangs dick on side of urinal to dry it.

Efficient: Waits until he has to crap and then does both.

Fat: Backs up and takes a blind shot at urinal, pisses on shoes.

Drunk: Holds left thumb in right hand, pisses in pants.

Conceited: Holds two inch dick like it is a baseball bat.

THE SCOTS

The Scotsman was on his way home from the pub when he came across a wee lad who was crying his eyes out.

'What's the matter, little boy?' he asked in a kindly voice.

'I've lost my penny,' wept the child.

'Don't cry lad. Here let me strike a match to help you to find it . . .'

Did you hear about the Scottish drunk who ran home behind the bus to save a dollar?

He could have run home behind a cab and saved a whole lot more.

The drunk from Edinburgh loved to play the bagpipes when he had had a few.

On his first trip to London he stayed at what he thought was a good hotel, but was not impressed.

On returning home he firmly declared that that would be the last time that he would venture down south.

'At three o'clock in the morning they hammered on my bedroom door,' he said.

'They even hammered on the floor and the ceiling. They hammered so loudly that I had great trouble hearing myself play the bagpipes.'

There is a great demand for thimbles in Scotland.
The Scots use them for shouting each other a whisky.

Did you hear about the Scot who fed his chickens the finest whisky?

He was sure that they would lay Scotch eggs.

A Scot will simply swallow the insult if you offer him a small glass of whisky.

Q. How do you torture a drunk Scot?
A. Nail his feet to the floor and play a Jimmy Shand record.

D octor, doctor, I can't stop stealing things.'
'Take these two pills after meals.'
'What if they don't work?'
'Then get me a crate of the best Scotch.'

A n American tourist found himself lost in the Scottish Highlands and had wandered around hopelessly for almost a week. On the seventh day he met an inebriated and kilted Scot.

'Thank God I've met you. I have been lost for a week and I am nearly done.'

'Is there a reward out for ye?' asked the Scot.

'No,' replied the American.

'Then I'm afraid ye are still lost.'

T wo Scots in a bar.
The first Scot asked his mate for a match.

When he had the match he began to search his pockets and said, 'I'm out of cigarettes as well.'

'In that case you won't be needing the match,' replied his mate.

Have you heard about the Scot who gave the waiter a tip? The horse lost.

An Irishman was up in front of the judge on a charge of being drunk and disorderly.

The judge asked him where he had bought his liquor.

'I didn't buy it, your honour, a Scotsman gave it to me.'

The judge banged down his gavel, 'Fourteen days for perjury,' he said.

Jock was a grand judge of a glass of Scotch whisky—and a merciless executioner.

The Scots drunk who was a little short on funds went into the barber shop enquiring about the prices.

'How much for a hair cut?'

'Twenty dollars.'

'How much for a shave?'

'Seven dollars, 50 cents.'

'In that case, shave my head.'

Did you hear about the two Scots drunks who got arrested after a smash and grab job?

They came back for their brick.

Jock was only five foot tall.

He attributed his shortness of stature to the fact that as a child in Scotland, he had been fed only condensed milk and shortbreads.

Q. What does a Scottish breakfast consist of?

A. A pound of steak, a bottle of whisky and an Alsatian dog.

The dog is to eat the steak.

Jock had been unemployed all his life and had given up any hope of ever finding a job.

His lack of income forced him into the situation of having to cadge drinks from all and sundry.

One day he had the luck to win a job with an Electric Company collecting money from the meters.

He was excited about the prospect of work and set off for his first day on the job with a mixture of excitement and anticipation.

That evening, after a day collecting the money, he was back in the bar shouting all round. He bought glasses of whisky for all the patrons.

'This is wonderful,' a friend shouted from across the bar. 'I suppose that it will be doubles all round when you get paid on Friday.'

'What?' answered Jock. 'Do I get paid as well . . .?'

The old aunt handed her grand nephew a glass of Scotch to celebrate the new year.

'This is a very old whisky,' said the lady, 'It is 100 years old.'

'Is that a fact? Mind you it's very small for its age.'

Two drunks bought a bottle of whisky for $2. It was the vilest stuff they had ever tasted.

'This is awful, I'll be glad when we've finished this,' one said to the other.

THE WIFE

A man drinks a shot of whiskey every night before bed. After years of this, the wife wants him to quit. She gets two shot glasses, filling one with water and the other with whiskey.

After getting him to the table that had the glasses, she brings his bait box. She says, 'I want you to see this.' She puts a worm in the water and it swims around.

She puts a worm in the whiskey and the worm dies immediately. She then says, feeling that she has made her point clear, 'What do you have to say about this experiment?'

He responds by saying: 'If I drink whiskey, I won't get worms!'

A businessman enters a tavern, sits down at the bar and orders a double martini on the rocks.

After he finishes the drink, he peeks inside his shirt pocket, then he asks the bartender to prepare another double martini.

After he finishes that one, he again peeks inside his shirt pocket and asks the bartender to bring another double martini.

The bartender says, 'Look, buddy, I'll bring martinis all night long. But you gotta tell me why you look inside your shirt pocket before every drink.'

The man replies, 'I'm peeking at a photo of my wife. When she starts to look good, then I know it's time to go home.'

These three guys are sitting at a bar arguing over which one has the ugliest wife.

The conversation begins to get heated to the point of the barkeeper telling them to get the hell out or shut up!

In fact he says, 'Why don't you settle it once and for all and just visit each other's house and decide for yourselves.'

'Damn good idea,' they agree, finish their drinks and make off for the first guy's house.

Upon arriving he bangs on his door and the wife answers. She's not pretty and he turns to collect the bet from the other two.

'Not so fast,' says the second, 'I got that beat.'

And off they go to his house. He bangs on the door and his wife comes to the door and all three step back in fright. She's damn ugly.

He asks to collect the bet but the third guy says, 'Sorry. I've got you both beat.'

He goes to his house and walks right in, there's no sign of anyone around.

He stomps his foot on the trap door in the floor and they all hear a voice say, 'Is that you honey?'

'Yeah it's me,' he says. 'Do you want me to come out?' she asks.

'Yes please,' he says.

'Should I put the bag on my head?' she asks.

He says, 'No. I don't want to screw you! I just want to show you off.'

A fellow in a bar notices that a woman, always alone, comes in on a fairly regular basis. After the second week, he made his move.

'No thank you.' she said politely. 'This may sound rather odd in this day and age, but I'm keeping myself pure until I meet the man I love.'

'That must be rather difficult,' the man replied.

'Oh, I don't mind too much.' she said. 'But, it has my husband pretty upset.'

A guy walks into a bar and sees his best friend sitting there, getting drunk.

When he asks what the problem is, the friend says 'When I make love to my wife, she just lays there. I've tried everything, but she doesn't moan, doesn't scream, doesn't even move.'

The guy pats his friend on the back and says 'Don't worry mate. The problem's not you. She does that with all of us.'

SAY THAT AGAIN?

A man walks into a bar and orders a beer.
He takes his first sip and sets it down. While he is looking around the bar, a monkey swings down and steals the pint of beer from him before he is able to stop the monkey.

The man asks the barman who owns the monkey. The barman replies the piano player.

The man walks over to the piano player and says, 'Do you know your monkey stole my beer.'

The pianist replies, 'No, but if you hum it, I'll play it.'

A guy walks into a bar and orders a beer. While the barman is pulling the brew, he hears a voice nearby him say, 'My goodness, you're looking handsome today.'

He looks up at the barman and says, 'Did you hear that?'

The barman says no.

The guy pays for his beer and thinks nothing further about it.

A few minutes later, he hears the voice again, this time it says, 'I really like the way you've done your hair, sexy.'

The guy spins around but no one is there. A little scared, the guy shakes his head and tells himself not to be silly.

Then he hears the voice for a third time, again from close by. 'You must be a real chick magnet you little spunk!'

The guy, freaking out now says, 'Hey, barman, I keep hearing this voice telling me how nice I look but there's no one around. Am I going out of my mind?'

'No, no,' replies the barman. 'That'd be the nuts . . . they're complimentary.'

A duck waddles into a bar and asks, 'Got any wasabe peas?' The bartender, a little perplexed tells the duck that his bar doesn't serve wasabe peas.

The next day the duck waddles in again, 'Got any wasabe peas?' he asks.

The barman again explains that his bar does not serve wasabe peas and furthermore it won't ever be serving wasabe peas so he can just piss off. The duck raises an eyebrow and walks out.

The following day the duck returns again. He's about to ask when the bartender interrupts forcefully, 'Listen duck face, we don't serve bloody wasabe peas. This is strictly a non-wasabe pea serving bar and you ask for wasabe peas in this bar again I'll nail your damn duck faced beak to the bar, now get outta here.'

The duck never heard such rudeness. He spun around and marched out.

The next day the duck waddles in and asks, 'Y'got any nails?'

A bit taken aback the barman answers, 'No.'

'Good,' says the duck, 'Got any wasabe peas?'

A short man walks in to the bar and begins to tell the bartender his story, 'Well, I wath driving down thith country road, when I thaw a thine that thaid "horth for thale."

'I jutht happened to be looking to buy a horth, tho I turned up the driveway to thee about it.

'The farmer wath quite nithe about thowing me the horth, but I made it clear to him that it had to be a healthy horth, not jutht any old thag back.

'The farmer told me it wath a three year old mare.

'When we got to the horth, I athked the farmer to pick me up to thee the hortheth eyth, becauth I wath too thort. The farmer reluctantly picked me up to thee.

'I checked the hortheth eyth and they theemed great and the farmer put me down. 'Nexthd, I athked the farmer to pick me up to thee the hortheth teeth. He wath even more reluctant thith time, but he did it.

'I grabbed the hortheth lipth, lifted them and tapped on the teeth to be thure they we tholid. They were and the farmer put me down.

'We thtepped back thowards the hortheth hind quarter, looking towardth hith head, when I athked the farmer to thee the hortheth twat.

'The farmer grabbed me, picked me up and thtuck me in the hortheth bum. Then he pulled me out and thtood me up, right at the back thide of the horth.

'Well, I wath in thock. I wath covered in poo and some got in my mouth.

'As I thpat it out, I thaid to the farmer, 'Let me rephrathe that. Can I thee her gallop thlowly . . .?'

THE STRESS OF IT ALL

A guy storms into a local bar and demands, 'Gimme a double of the strongest whiskey you got! I'm so pissed I can't even see straight!'

The bartender, noticing that the little man is a bit the worse for wear, pours him a double.

The man swills down the drink and says, 'Gimme another one.'

The bartender pours the drink, but says, 'Now, before I give you this, why don't you let off a little steam and tell me why you're so upset?'

So the man relates the following story, 'Well, I was sitting in the bar next door when this gorgeous blonde slinks in and sits beside me at the bar. Well, a couple of minutes later she leans over, licks my ear and asks if I'm interested? I say sure, so she grabs my hand and we leave. She took me down the street here to a nice hotel and up to her room. As soon as she shut the door she slips out of her dress and I get out of my clothes. As soon as we jumped into the bed, I hear some keys jingling and someone starts fumbling with the door. The blonde says, "Oh my god, it's my boyfriend. He must have lost his boxing match tonight, he's gonna be real mad. Quick, hide." 'So, I opened the wardrobe, but I figured that was probably the first place he would look, so I didn't hide there. Then I looked under the bed, but no, I figured he's bound to look there also. By now I could hear the key in the lock. I noticed the window was open, so I climbed out and was hanging there by my fingers praying that the guy would not see me.

'I hear the guy finally get the door open and he yells out, "Who you been sleeping with now?" The girl says, "Nobody, honey, now come to bed and calm down." Well the guy starts tearing up the room. I hear him tear the door off the closet and throw it across the room. I'm thinking "Boy, I'm glad I didn't hide in there." Then I hear him lift up the bed and throw it across the room. Good thing I didn't hide under there either. Then I heard him say, "What's that over there by the window?" I think "Oh God, I'm dead meat now." But the blonde by now is trying real hard to distract him and convince him to stop looking. Well, I hear the guy go into the bathroom and I hear water running for a long time and I figure maybe he's gonna take a bath or something, when all of a sudden he leans out and pours a pitcher of scalding hot water out of the window right on top of my head! I mean look at this, I got second degree burns all over my scalp and shoulders. Now that didn't really bother me. Next the guy starts slamming the window shut over and over on my hands. I mean, look at my fingers. They're a bloody mess, I can hardly hold onto this glass. But that was not the worst part.'

The bartender then says, 'That all sounds pretty bad, what could be worse?'

'Well I was hanging there and I turned around and looked down and I was only about six inches off the ground!'

This bear goes into a bar and asks for a beer.
The barman says, 'Sorry, we don't serve beers to bears in this bar.'

The bear bangs on the bar.

The barman says, 'Sorry, we don't serve beers to bears in this bar, especially not bears who bang on bars.'

The bear grabs a passing barmaid and bashes her.

The barman says, 'Sorry, we don't serve beers to bears in this bar, especially not bears who bang on bars and bash barmaids.'

The bear bellows at the other barman to bring him a beer.

The barman says, 'Sorry, we don't serve beers to bears in this bar, especially not bears who bang on bars, bash barmaids and bellow at barmen.'

In exasperation, the bear bites the bar.

The barman says, 'Sorry, we don't serve bears who are on drugs.'

The bear says, 'On drugs? I'm not on drugs.'

The barman says, 'Look bear, I saw the bar-bit-u-ate.'

THEN THERE WAS . . .

Two fat blokes sitting in a pub.
One says to the other, 'Your round.'
And the other replies, 'So are you, yer fat bastard!'

A man walks into a bar carrying a small box. He says to the bartender, 'How much do you think I could make from a dancing fly?'

'A dancing fly?' says the bartender, 'Let me see it.'

The man opens the box and puts a tiny fly onto the bar, goes over and turns on the jukebox and straight away the fly begins to dance.

'Hey that's pretty good,' says the bartender, 'How long did it take to teach him that?'

'Ten years,' replies the man 'Do you know an agent who could help me make him a star?'

'Sure,' says the bartender, 'See that man over there on the phone? He's in the entertainment game.'

The man puts the fly back in the box, walks over and carefully puts the fly on the table next to the phone and patiently waits for the man to hang up.

'Yes, of course I will,' says the bloke on the phone. 'No, I won't forget. Okay, thank you, see you.'

Bang he goes with the phone on the table.

'Blasted bugs,' he says. 'Now what is it you want?'

A group of loud and rowdy drunks make a hell of a racket in the street after a big, big night on the turps at the pub.

It is still the wee small hours of the morning and the lady of the house flings open a window and shouts at them to keep quiet.

'Is this where George lives?' one of the drunks asks.

'Yes, it is,' the woman replies.

'Well then,' says the drunk, 'Could you come and pick him out so the rest of us can go home?'

AMAZING SCENES

A man walks into a bar and says, 'Bartender, give me two shots. One for me and one for my best mate.'

The barman says, 'You want them both now or do you want me to wait until your buddy arrives to pour his?'

The guy says, 'Oh, I want them both now. I've got my best mate in my pocket here.' He then pulls a little three inch man out of his pocket. The bartender asks, 'You mean to say, he can drink that much?'

'Oh, sure. He can drink it all and then some,' the man retorted.

So, the barman pours the two shots and sure enough, the little guy drinks it all up.

'That's amazing!' says the bartender. 'What else can he do? Can he walk?'

The man flicks a ten buck note down to the end of the bar and says, 'Hey, Rodney, go fetch that note.'

The little guy runs down to the end of the bar, picks up the note and runs back down and gives it to the man.

The barman is in total shock. 'That's amazing!' he says. 'What else can he do? Does he talk?'

The man looks up at the barman with a look of surprise in his eye and says, 'Talk? Sure he talks. Hey, Rodney, tell him about that time we were in Africa, on safari and you called that Witch Doctor a dickhead!'

A father and son walk into a pub. The son has no arms, no legs, no torso. In fact he is just a head.

The father explains to the barman that he's a terrific young lad, who hasn't let his obvious disability hinder his achievements.

He goes on to explain that today is his son's eighteenth birthday and that he wants to buy him his first beer.

The barman raises an eyebrow but obliges the father and serves them a beer each.

The father pats his son on the crown and pops a straw in his mouth.

The young lad takes his first sip and, WHOP, a neck and torso pop out from beneath him.

The wide-eyed father encourages his son to take another sip.

The lad does so and, WHOP, two arms pop out.

The father, now hysterical with joy, demands the boy sip again.

The whole bar gathers to watch the phenomenon. He sips and sure enough two legs pop out.

Slowly, he staggers to his feet. He takes a couple of tentative steps, then walks around the bar, then runs out of the pub and onto the road where he is hit by a bus and instantly killed.

The barman shakes his head, turns to the devastated father and says, 'He should've quit while he was ahead.'

A Jelly Baby walks into a bar and starts talking to a Smartie. After a few beers the Smartie says, 'Hey, a bunch of us are heading to that new club, fancy tagging along?'

The Jelly Baby says, 'No mate, I'm a soft centre, I always end up getting my head kicked in.'

So Smartie says, 'Don't worry about it, I'm a bit of a hard case, I'll look after you.'

Jelly Baby thinks about it for a minute and says, 'Fair enough, as long as you'll look after me,' and off they go.

After a few more beers in the club, three Lozenges walk in.

As soon as he sees them, Smartie hides under the table.

The Lozenges take one look at Jelly Baby and start kicking him, breaking bottles over his little jelly head, smashing him with little sugary chairs and generally having a laugh.

After a while they get bored and walk out.

Jelly Baby pulls his battered Jelly Baby body over to the

table and wipes up his Jelly Baby blood and turns to Smartie and says, 'I thought you were going to look after me.'

'Oooh, I would have!' says Smartie, 'But those Lozenges are bloody menthol . . .'

A guy walks in a bar and buys a huge beer.
Then he sees someone he knows and decides to go and say hi to them, but he does not want to drag his beer mug with him.

So he sets it on a table, along with a note 'I spat in this beer', hoping that nobody will steal it.

Upon return, he sees another note saying 'Me too!'

TOO LONG?

SIGNS THAT YOU SPEND TOO MUCH TIME IN THE PUB INCLUDE:

- You lose arguments with inanimate objects.
- You have to hold onto the lawn to keep from falling off the earth.
- Your job is interfering with your drinking.
- Your doctor finds traces of blood in your alcohol stream.
- The back of your head keeps getting hit by the toilet seat.
- You sincerely believe alcohol to be the elusive fifth food group.
- Twenty-four hours in a day, 24 beers in a case—coincidence??—I think not!
- You can focus better with one eye closed.
- The parking lot seems to have moved while you were in the bar.
- Your twin sons are named Barley and Hops.
- Mosquitoes catch a buzz after attacking you.
- At AA meetings you begin, 'Hi, my name is . . . uh . . .'
- Your idea of cutting back is less salt.
- The whole bar says 'Hi,' when you come in . . .

FOOLISH BEHAVIOUR

These two hunters enter the bar every day, the first one always carries the skin of a bear, the other one is always empty handed.

So the second one goes up to the first hunter and asks him how he gets to shoot a bear every day.

'Well, that's easy,' he replies, 'I just go over to one of those holes in the mountain, stand in front of it and shout, "Yo, fat ass of a bear, get your stinking ass out off this hole!" as loud as I can. Then the bear gets out and I shoot it. Easy as that.'

'Okay,' the other one says, 'I'll remember that.' So the next day, the first hunter comes into the bar with his skin and orders a beer.

About ten minutes later, the second one crawls in, covered in blood, missing a leg and is generally a mess.

So the other hunter yells, 'What happened to you man?'

'Aargh,' says the other one, 'I did what you told me to do, I went to a hole, started shouting and swearing at that bear and guess what happened?'

'What?'

'A train came out.'

This posh Pommy bloke is travelling through Queensland in the middle of summer by bicycle and is caught in a huge tropical storm.

He sees a sign which says there is a pub 30 kilometres up the road. So he rides his bike to the pub and when he finally gets there his appearance resembles that of a drowned rat.

Anyway, the locals hardly even look up from their beers as he walks in, dripping wet and heads up to the bar and orders a scotch on ice.

The barman gives him the worst scotch he has ever tasted, but the pommy drinks it down and asks the barman where the dunny is.

The barman tells him it's outside.

So the pommy trudges outside into the rain and all he can see in the rain is two big piles of shit, one much bigger than the other.

So the pommy walks over to the smaller pile, relieved that someone had the sense to start a new pile, since the larger one was clearly unmanageable.

He has his pants around his ankles and is in the process of relieving himself when a gunshot rings out and a bullet smacks into the heap just beside his head.

Well the poor pommy turns around, in a somewhat vulnerable position and sees this huge Aussie guy standing at the door of the pub with his still smoking gun in his hand.

'What. What is going on?' stammers the poor pommy.

The huge Aussie responds, 'Get the hell out of the Ladies you dirty bastard.'

SMARTER THAN YOU THINK

At a pub in the country, one of the favourite pastimes of the patrons was to offer the village simpleton the choice between a shiny new 50 cent piece and a shaggy old ten dollar note.

The young lad would deliberate and think about it but, in the end, he always chose the shiny new coin.

As the story of the lad and his inevitable choices became known around the district, more people came to the pub to have a laugh at the boy's expense.

Bus tours would stop by the pub and the tourists would get out and offer the boy the choice of the shiny coin or the battered note.

He always chose the coin.

His uncle, who was fond of the boy, had had enough of their smug laughter and took the lad aside.

'Jimmy, I just don't understand. You are not as silly as you make out and I'm sure you know the difference in value between a 50 cent piece and a ten dollar note. Why do you keep choosing the fifty cents?'

'Well, uncle, it's like this. How long do you think this choosing business would go on once I choose the ten dollar note? Nobody would offer me the bloody coin again . . .'

Did you hear about the drunk with the gambling problem? He denied he had a problem and made a bet that he could give it up.

The drunk never shed a tear when his wife of 40 years died suddenly.

He was in the pub shortly after having a quiet ale, when his mate asked him how he was coping.

'Oh, I'm over it all now,' he said, 'It isn't as if she was a blood relation.'

Two drunks were on a train heading home.

'You know, privatisation of the railways was one of the best things that ever happened.'

'I agree. You're going to Melbourne and I'm going to Sydney.'

The man was sick of his wife and her 'know it all' attitude.

He came home late from the pub with a couple of his mates and hatched a plot.

'Give me a hand to get this pig out of the van,' he asked.

After they had done that he asked them to hold the front door while he got the pig inside the house.

'Now, I will need your help to get the animal upstairs and into the bath,' he begged.

'Look here,' said his mates, 'We don't mind helping you out, but what the hell is going on here?'

'Okay, you're entitled to an explanation. You know how Jeanie always knows everything. Every time I tell her something, she says "yes I know." looks bored and turns away from me. Well, I have had enough. It's time for her to experience a little of her own medicine. When she comes to me and tells me that there's a big hairy pig in the bath, I am simply going to roll over and say, "I know".'

An Englishman was holding forth at the bar.

'I was born an Englishman. All my life I have been an Englishman and when I die I shall die an Englishman.'

An Irish voice from the other end of the bar piped in with, 'Have you no ambition, then?'

A drunk was telling the whole bar about his lineage.
'I can trace my line right back to Noah's ark,' he boasted.

Not to be outdone, another drinker came in with, 'At the time of the great floods, my family had their own boat.'

During outbreaks of fever it is wise to filter and boil your drinking water.

Just to be on the safe side, however, drink whisky.

The parson was in full flight.
'When judgement day comes,' he thundered, 'There will be weeping and gnashing of teeth.'

'I don't have teeth,' called a drunk who had slunk into the back seat for a little shelter.

'Teeth will be provided,' returned the minister.

The wife returned from shopping with provisions for the week, six bottles of whisky and a loaf of bread.

Her husband shouted at her angrily, 'What in the name of the lord did you bring all that bread for, woman?'

The drunk was on a train and next to him sat a clergy man. He pulled out a bottle of whisky in a brown paper bag and took a drink from it.

Unable to contain himself, the reverend said, 'I'm 65 years old and never a drop of that stuff has passed my lips.'

'And it won't today either,' replied the drunk taking another swig.

The drunk fell into the huge tank containing half a dozen man eating sharks.

He survived the ordeal because he was wearing a t-shirt which read 'England for the World Cup.'

Not even the sharks would swallow that!

The drunk arrived at the parson's home late at night in a state of considerable intoxication.

'Reverend,' he said, 'I'm worried about the doctrine of predetermination.'

'Look,' said the minister, 'Why don't you come back when you are sober?'

'Because, when I'm sober, I don't give a shit about predetermination.'

Two young football fans were travelling to Rome to support their team and were making arrangements as to where to meet.

'Let's meet at the Vatican,' said the first.

'In the bar or the lounge?' asked the second.

The weekly bar raffle was won by a patron who had never won anything in his life before.

The prize was a toilet brush.

Mid-week and he was back in the bar when the barman asked, 'And how do you like your new toilet brush?'

'Well I don't like it much at all. I think I'll go back to using toilet paper.'

Q. Have you heard about the drunk who was suffering from alcoholic constipation?
A. He couldn't pass a pub.

One drunk to another:
'My wife is a sex object. Every time I want sex, she objects.'

The drunk in a fever of religious fervour and full of the drink, hurled a bottle of bleach through the side door of the local church.

He was fined for bleach of the priest.

Three mates had enjoyed drinking in the same place at the same pub for many years.

One day, one of them came with the bad news that he was not long for this world and that when he died he would like them all to buy him a whisky and pour it on his grave.

There was silence as his mates contemplated the idea.

Then one spoke.

'Would it not be better if we gave it a good swill around our kidney first?'

The wife awoke to the sound of her husband searching clumsily around the room, knocking furniture about.

'What are you looking for?' she asked.

'Nothing,' came the reply.

'Then you'll find it in the whisky bottle.'

The fisherman died and was met by St Peter at the pearly gates.

'You have told too many lies to get in here,' said St Peter.

'Have a heart,' came the reply, 'You were a fisherman once yourself.'

A drunk who was down on his luck phoned up a friend and asked for a loan of ten pounds.

'Sorry! You'll have to speak up, I can't hear what you're saying,' said the friend.

'Can you lend me ten pounds?'

'I'm terribly sorry but the line is noisy, I can' hear a word you're saying.'

At this stage the operator chipped in with, 'There's nothing wrong with the line. I can hear everything quite distinctly.'

'In that case, you can lend him the ten quid.'

Two mates were doing a quiz at the bar.

The question was, 'If you have 33 dollars in one pocket and 61 dollars in the other, what would you have?'

'Somebody else's trousers,' was the reply.

The second question was, 'If the Tate Gallery was on fire and you had the opportunity to save one painting, which one would you save?'

'The one closest to the door.'

The third question was, 'If you had five pounds and I asked you for three. How much would you have?'

'Five.'

Graffiti on a wall
DRINK IS YOUR ENEMY
Written next to it
LOVE YOUR ENEMY

An Englishman, an Irishman and a Scotsman went to the pub together.

The Englishman spent ten pounds, the Irishman spent seven pounds and the Scot had an excellent afternoon out.

The drunk carried his inebriated mate into an AA Meeting.

'He's drunk. You can't bring him in here. This is an AA Meeting.'

'Don't worry. He's far too drunk to notice.'

THE WILD
WEST HOTEL

The Lone Ranger and Tonto are having a beer at the saloon when a cowboy marches in and says, 'Who owns that big black horse tied out the front?'

'I do,' the Lone Ranger replied, 'Why?'

The cowboy drawled, 'You better take care of him. He's almost dead from the heat.'

The Lone Ranger and Tonto rushed outside and found Silver leaning against the hitching post, panting. They got him some water and soon Silver was looking better, but he was still panting.

The Lone Ranger said, 'Tonto, run around Silver as fast as you can and see if the breeze makes him feel any better.'

Tonto replied, 'Sure, Kemosabe', and began running around and around Silver. The Lone Ranger returned to the bar to finish his beer.

A few minutes later, another cowboy came into the bar and drawled, 'Who owns that big white horse outside?'

'I do,' the Lone Ranger said, 'What's wrong with him this time?'

'Nothin',' the cowboy said, 'But you left your Injun running.'

An Indian scouting party rides into town, captures a cowboy from the local saloon and brings him back to their camp to meet the chief.

The chief says to the cowboy, 'You going die. But we sorry for you, so give you one wish a day for three days. At sundown third day, you die. What first wish?'

The cowboy says, 'I want to see my horse.'

The Indians get his horse. The cowboy grabs the horse's ear and whispers something, then slaps the horse on the back. The horse takes off. Two hours later, the horse comes back with a naked blonde.

She jumps off the horse and goes into the tepee with the cowboy.

The Indians look at each other, figuring, 'Typical white man . . . only think one thing.' The second day, the chief says, 'What wish today?'

The cowboy says, 'I want to see my horse again.'

The Indians bring him his horse. The cowboy leans over to the horse and whispers something in the horse's ear, then slaps it on the back. Two hours later, the horse comes back with a naked redhead. She gets off and goes in the tepee with the cowboy.

The Indians shake their heads, figuring, 'Typical white man—going die tomorrow, but can only think one thing.'

The last day comes and the chief says, 'This last wish, white man. What want?'

The cowboy says, 'I want to see my horse again.'

The Indians bring him his horse.

The cowboy grabs the horse by both ears, twists them hard and yells, 'Read my lips you idiot! POSSE, damn it! P-O-S-S-E!'

A guy travelling through the prairies of the USA stopped at a small town and went to a bar.

He stood at the end of the bar and lit up a cigar. As he sipped his drink, he stood there quietly blowing smoke rings.

After he blew nine or ten smoke rings into the air, an angry American Indian approached him and said, 'Now listen buddy, if you don't stop calling me that I'll kick your head in.'

THE SIZE OF IT ALL

A man walks into a bar and starts pouring down the beers. Having had one too many, the man was beginning to display an ugly side.

An unescorted female sat down beside him and he whispered to her, 'Hey, burp! How about it babe? You and me?'

As she got up to move, he said loudly, 'Honey, you sure look like you could use the money, but I don't have an extra two dollars.'

She looked back and replied just as loudly, 'What makes you think I charge by the inch?'

Joe falls madly in love with this bartender named Wendy, so he gets her name tattooed on his penis.

She breaks up with him, though and he's so devastated that he goes away on a Caribbean singles cruise to try to get her off his mind.

He drinks away his troubles at the bar on the cruise ship and one night drinks so many beers his bladder is about to explode.

So he goes into the bathroom and takes the urinal right next to this muscular black man.

Joe takes a glance at the guy's penis and sees the word 'WENDY' tattooed on it. He says, 'Hey, you knew Wendy too?'

The black guy turns to him and says, 'No, mun, when I get hard it says 'WELCOME TO JAMAICA, HAVE A NICE DAY.'

WELL, HELLO . . .

PUB PICK-UP LINES THAT MAY OR MAY NOT WORK

Here's some suggested opening lines for the next time you are at the pub and you see Mr or Ms Right at the adjoining seat.

(But be careful if you are wearing the Beer Goggles.)

- I wish you were a door so I could bang you all day long.
- Nice legs. What time do they open?
- Do you work for the post office? I thought I saw you checking out my package.
- You have 206 bones in your body, want one more?
- I'm a bird watcher and I'm looking for a Big Breasted Bed thrasher, have you seen one?
- I'm fighting the urge to make you the happiest woman on earth tonight. I'd really like to see how you look when I'm naked.
- You must be the limp doctor because I've got a stiffy.
- You know, if I were you, I'd have sex with me.
- You, me, whipped cream and handcuffs. Any questions?
- Those clothes would look great in a crumpled heap on my bedroom floor.
- Hi, the voices in my head told me to come over and talk to you.
- (Lick finger and wipe on her shirt.) 'Let's get you out of those wet clothes.'

TWO ETHNIC TYPES MEET AND . . .

A Jew and a Chinese are in the pub together. The Jew stands up and gives the Chinaman a tremendous slap.

'What are you doing?' says the stricken Chinese.

'That's for Pearl-Harbor,' says the Jew.

'But I am Chinese! The Japanese were responsible for that!' says the Chinese.

'Japanese, Chinese—all the same.'

They resume their seats. Time passes.

The Chinaman gets up and kicks the Jew.

'Hey! What's going on?'

'That's for the Titanic!' says the Chinese.

'But the Titanic was hit by an Iceberg!'

'Iceberg, Weissberg. All the same.'

A priest, a minister and a rabbi are in a bar. The priest says, 'Let's draw a circle on the ground and throw our money into the air. Whatever lands outside the circle, we keep. Whatever lands inside the circle, we give to God.'

The minister says, 'I have a better idea: we only keep what lands inside the circle.'

The Rabbi says, 'Tell you what, let's just throw the money up and whatever God wants, he can keep.'

Three construction contractors are in a pub—a Black, a Jew and an Italian.

A man approaches them and says he has a job—some

gates are in need of some repair and he wanted some estimates.

The Black contractor looked the job over carefully and estimated the job at $600. When asked how he came up with that figure, he said, '$200 materials, $200 labour and $200 profit.'

The client then asked the Jewish contractor for an estimate. After careful inspection the Jew answered, '$3000–$1000 materials, $1000 labour and $1000 profit.'

When the client asked the Italian for an estimate, he answered immediately without looking over the job at all—$2600.

Asked how he came up with that figure he answered, 'Simple, $1000 for you, $1000 for me and $600 to get the lowest bidder over there to do the work.'

A kilted Scotsman was walking down a country path after finishing off a considerable amount of whisky at a local pub.

As he staggered down the road, he felt quite sleepy and decided to take a nap, with his back against a tree.

As he slept, two young lasses walked down the road and heard the Scotsman snoring loudly. They saw him and one said, 'I've always wondered what a Scotsman wears under his kilt.'

She boldly walked over to the sleeping man, raised his kilt and saw what nature had provided him at his birth.

Her friend said, 'Well, he has solved a great mystery for us, now! He must be rewarded!' So, she took a blue ribbon from her hair and gently tied it around what nature had provided the Scotsman and the two walked away.

Several minutes later, the Scotsman was awakened by the call of nature and walked around to the other side of the tree to relieve himself. He raised his kilt . . . and saw where the blue ribbon was tied. After several moments of bewilderment, the Scotsman said . . .

'I dinna know where y'been lad . . . but it's nice ta'know y'won first prize!'

Three Irish Catholic ladies are having a quiet drink in a pub across the street from a brothel.

'Isn't that Reverend Brown coming out of there?'

'What a scandal! For a clergyman to sink like that!'

'Isn't that Rabbi Armlestein?'

'Oh, that filthy man! Disgusting!'

'Isn't that Father Murphy?'

'My, my, there must be a very sick girl in there.'

A bloke used to loudly tell dirty jokes in the bar every night—much to the distress of women patrons.

The women wanted to do something about it.

So they decided that the next time that he started with these kind of jokes, they would leave the bar as a protest.

Somehow the man heard about the plan.

The next night, he started, 'In Sweden, a prostitute makes $2000 per night.'

All the women stand up and start to leave the class.

He shouts after them, 'Where are you going? The plane to Sweden doesn't take off until the day after tomorrow.'

There are two men who work at a sexual paraphernalia store. The older man decides to go to lunch down the pub about noon and asks his partner to watch the shop.

The other consents. Shortly after the first man leaves, a white woman comes into the store looking for a dildo.

The man is happy to help her and sells her one about six inches long.

After she leaves, a black woman comes in looking for a dildo and again the man is happy to help her and sells her one 10 inches long.

Finally, after the second woman leaves, a Polish woman comes in the store looking for something really huge.

The man knows exactly what she's looking for and sells her a large silver one.

After lunch is over, the first man returns and asks how was

business. The second man says, 'Great! I sold two dildos and my thermos!'

A bar customer asked the bartender if he wanted to hear a Polack joke.

The bartender pointed to a large man at the end of the bar and said, 'He's Polish.'

Then the bartender pointed to a burly policeman near the door and repeated, 'He's Polish.'

The bartender finished, 'Now, think about whether you want to tell that joke, because I'm Polish, too.'

The customer replied, 'I guess I won't tell that joke after all. I'd have to explain it three times.'

A Russian and an American are talking in a bar.

'When I'm in a good mood I drive a car that is painted a light colour,' says the American. 'When I'm busy or have a lot of troubles, I drive a darker coloured car. And when I go for vacation overseas, I pick a brightly coloured car.'

'Things are much easier in Russia,' says the Russian.

'If you are in a good mood, they will give you a ride in yellow car with a blue stripe. If you feel bad, the car will be white and the stripe red. And I was abroad only once and there I drove a tank . . .'

Rabbi, what should I do? My son has converted to
Christianity.'

'I don't know,' answered the Rabbi. 'Come back tomorrow
and I'll ask advice from God.'
The man comes back the next day.

'I can't help you,' says the Rabbi.

'God told me he has the same problem.'

A young English girl meets an American guy in the pub.
To try and impress him, she says, 'My genealogy starts from
a person who met the Queen. She touched his shoulder and
made him a knight.'

'Well', said the American, 'My genealogy starts from a person
who faced an Indian chief. The chief touched his head with a
tomahawk and made him an angel.'

An American physician meets a Russian colleague in the bar.
'Is it true,' says the American, 'That there are cases in your
country where a patient was treated for one disease, only to
have the autopsy reveal another cause of death?'

'Absolutely not. All our patients die from the diseases we
treat them for.'

LAWYERS

A man stomps into a bar, obviously angry.
He growls at the bartender, 'Gimme a beer', takes a slug and shouts out, 'All lawyers are assholes!'

A guy at the other end of the bar retorts, 'You take that back!'

The angry man snarls, 'Why? Are you a lawyer?'

The guy replies, 'No, I'm an asshole!'

A t a convention of biological scientists in a hotel, one researcher remarks to another over a drink in the bar, 'Did you know that in our lab we have switched from mice to lawyers for our experiments?'

'Really?' the other replied, 'Why did you switch?'

'Well, for three reasons. First we found that lawyers are far more plentiful, second, the lab assistants don't get so attached to them and thirdly there are some things even a rat won't do . . .'

A very successful lawyer parked his brand new Lexus in front of the pub, ready to show it off to his drinking mates.

As he got out, a truck passed too close and completely tore the door off of the driver's side. The counsellor immediately grabbed his cell phone, dialled 911 and within minutes a policeman pulled up.

Before the officer had a chance to ask any questions, the lawyer started screaming hysterically. His Lexus, which he had just picked up the day before, was now completely ruined and would never be the same, no matter what the body shop did to it.

When the lawyer finally wound down from his ranting and raving, the officer shook his head in disgust and disbelief.

'I can't believe how materialistic you lawyers are,' he said.

'You are so focused on your possessions that you don't notice anything else.'

'How can you say such a thing?' asked the lawyer.

The cop replied, 'Don't you know that your left arm is missing from the elbow down? It must have been torn off when the truck hit you.'

'Ah!' screamed the lawyer. 'Where's my Rolex!'

A man is having a few quiet drinks in a bar, when a bloke walks up to him and says, 'Do you want a new brain?'

'What? A new brain?'

'I'm not kidding,' the bloke says. 'I've worked out this technique of making spare brains. I can swap for your old one or do a trade-up.'

'Oh, okay. So how much for engineer brain?'

'Three dollars for 100 grams.'

'How much for doctor brain?'

'Four dollars for 100 grams.'

'How much for lawyer brain?'

'One hundred dollars for 50 grams.'

'Why is lawyer brain so much more?'

'Do you know how many lawyers you need to kill to get one ounce of brain?'

A rabbit and a snake, both blind from birth, happen to meet in the pub one day.

They began talking and the rabbit asked the snake, 'Would you mind running your hands over my body and telling me what kind of an animal I am? I'm too embarrassed to ask my near-sighted friends because I'm afraid they'll make fun of me.'

The snake said, 'Okay,' and proceeded to wind himself around the rabbit from one end to the other, then back again.

'Well,' the snake said, 'You're kind of warm with real soft fur and you have two very long, furry ears.'

The rabbit thought about that for a moment and then exclaimed, 'Wow! I must be a bunny!'

And he hopped around and hopped around and starts to hop away.

'Wait!' shouted the snake, 'What about me? Come back here and do the same thing for me!'

The rabbit hopped over and with his fury little paws, patted the snake from one end to the other and then back again.

He sat down without saying a word.

'Well?' asks the snake, 'What kind of animal am I?'

'I'm not really sure,' said the rabbit.

'You're kind of cold and slimy and for the life of me, I can't tell your head from your ass.'

The snake thinks and thinks about this, then exclaims, 'Wow! I must be a lawyer.'

BAR TRICKS

Each time Craig visits this bar he has a little white box with him.

The bargirl is finally overcome with interest and asks, 'What's in the box?' To which Craig replies 'The most amazing frog ever. He loves to go down on women and he is really great.'

She suggests that she would like to find out just how good the frog is.

In the back room she takes off all her clothes and spreads her legs apart as the man takes the frog out of the box and places him between her legs.

After several minutes nothing is happening.

The man reaches down and picks the frog up and shaking him says, 'Now listen, I am going to show you how one more time . . .!'

Two guys are sitting in a bar getting pretty loaded. Suddenly, one of them throws up all over himself.

'Aw man, my wife is going to kill me when she sees this,' he says.

His buddy replies, 'Don't worry about it. That happened to me before.

'Here's what you do. Put a $20 bill in your pants pocket. When you get home, tell your wife that some drunk threw up on you and he gave you the 20 to pay for the cleaning, okay?'

'All right, I'll try it.'

So he goes home and his wife immediately starts bitching about his suit. 'Now look what you've done to yourself!'

'No, no, honey,' he slurs back. 'Some drunk guy puked on me, but he gave me this twenty bucks to get my suit cleaned.'

With that he reaches into his pocket and throws the money on the table.

His wife looks at it and says, 'I thought that you said he only gave you $20. How come there's $40 here?'

The man slurs back, 'He shit in my pants, too.'

GOODLINESS

A man was walking home one night when he bumped into a beautiful woman.

They were talking for a few hours and the woman seemed really interested.

The woman then came to the subject of smoking, drinking, swearing and lying and that she disapproved of them.

She told the man that she had never met another man that has told her the truth.

The man, knowing that the woman was interested, started to lie.

He told her he had never smoked, drank or swore.

Later that night the woman was so impressed with the man, she took him home with her.

After they had made wild passionate love, the man reached over to his jeans, which were on the floor beside the bed.

He was looking through his pockets, but didn't seem to be finding what he wanted. The woman then asked him what was the matter?

He turn around, looked at her and said, 'Ah, shit, I left my friggin' fags at the bloody pub!'

A fellow walks into a bar very down on himself. As he walks up to the bar the bartender asks, 'What's the matter?'

The fellow replies, 'Well I've got these two horses and well . . . I can't tell them apart. I don't know if I'm mixing up riding times or even feeding them the right foods.'

The bartender, feeling sorry for the guy, tries to think of something he can do.

'Why don't you try shaving the tail of one of the horses?'

The man stops crying and says, 'That sounds like a good idea, I think I'll try it.'

A few months later, he comes back to the bar in worse condition than he was before.

'What's the matter now?' the bartender asks.

The fellow, in no condition to be in public, answers, 'I shaved the tail of one of the horses but it grew back and I can't tell them apart again!'

The bartender, now just wanting him to shut up or leave says, 'Why don't you try shaving the mane, maybe that will not grow back.'

The fellow stops crying, has a few drinks and leaves.

A few months later, the fellow is back in the bar. The bartender has never seen anybody in this sorry a state.

Without the bartender even asking, the fellow breaks into his problems. 'I . . . I shaved the mane of one of the horses and . . . it . . . it . . . grew back. And I can't tell the difference again.'

The bartender, now furious at the guy's general stupidity, yells, 'For crying out loud, just measure the stupid horses. Perhaps one is slightly taller that the other one!'

The fellow looks up. Inspiration! He cannot believe what the bartender has said and storms out of the bar.

The next day the fellow comes running back into the bar as if he had just won the lottery.

'It worked, it worked!' he exclaims.

'I measured the horses and the black one is two inches taller than the white one . . .!'

OOH-ERR . . .!

This homeless guy walks into a bar and says, 'Gimme whiskey.'

The bartender says, 'I'll have to see your money first.'

'I'm broke, sonny, but if you give me a bottle of whiskey, I'll get up on that stage and fart the national anthem!'

The bartender had never seen someone fart any kind of song, so he agrees.

The homeless guy drinks the whole bottle of whiskey, then staggers up on stage and the audience starts applauding.

Then he drops his pants and the audience starts cheering even louder.

Then, he proceeds to shit all over the stage and everyone gets so disgusted and leaves.

The bartender screams, 'You said you were gonna fart the national anthem! Not shit all over my stage!'

The guy replies, 'Hey! Even Dame Nellie has to clear her throat before she sings!'

A guy has to take a crap really bad, so he goes into a bar. He thinks the bathroom is upstairs, so he goes upstairs. He can't find the bathroom anywhere, but he finds a hole in the floor so he takes a crap in it.

After that he goes downstairs and there's no one down there, so he asks the bartender were everyone is and he says 'Where the hell were you when the shit hit the fan?'

Three women were sitting at a bar talking about how loose they were. The first one said, 'My boyfriend can fit his fist up there.'

The second one says, 'My boyfriend can fit his arm up there.'

The third just laughed and slid down the bar stool.

One day, having been down a shaft in Lightning Ridge for three weeks, a lonesome miner came into the first pub he saw. 'I'm lookin' for the meanest, roughest and toughest whore in town!' he said to the bartender.

'Well, we got her!' replied the barman. 'She's upstairs in the second room on the right.' The miner handed the bartender a handful of opals to pay for the whore and two bottles of beer.

He grabbed the bottles, stomped up the stairs, kicked open the second door on the right and yelled, 'I'm lookin' for the meanest, roughest and toughest whore in the town!'

The woman inside the room looked at the miner and said, 'You found her!' Then she stripped naked, bent over and grabbed her ankles.

'How do you know I want to do it in that position?' asked the miner.

'I don't,' replied the whore, 'But I thought you might like to open those beers first.'

A little guy bustles his way up to a crowded bar.
He's been on his feet all day and wants to sit down so he asks the bartender if there's anywhere he can sit.

The bartender gets up on the bar, drops his dacks and takes a shit right there on the bar.

The little guy is shocked, 'What the hell is that?'

The barman answers, 'It's a bar stool.'

A guy walks into a bar and his ears start leaking.
The smell is so bad that the patrons have to clear the bar.

The barman approaches the man and says, 'What'll it be, shit for brains?'

Two condoms are walking past a gay bar. One turns to the other and says 'Wanna go get shit faced?'

A fella in his hospital bed keeps ringing for the nurse because he has to take a dump really bad.

He can't hold it any more and finally messes in his bed. To clean it up, he pulls the sheet off the bed, wads it up and tosses it out the window.

Joe, the local drunkard, is on his way to his favourite haunt when this sheet happens to land square on his head.

He staggers into the bar and the bartender, taking one look and getting a whiff, says, 'Joe, you smell awful.'

Joe says, 'You would too, if you just beat the shit out of a ghost.'

Two cannibals are eating their dinner at the jungle pub and one cannibal says to the other,

'I don't like my mother-in-law much.'

The other cannibal replies, 'Well, just eat your chips then!'

RELATIONSHIPS

A woman announces to her friend at the pub that she is getting married for the fourth time.

'How wonderful! But I hope you don't mind me asking what happened to your first husband?'

'He ate poisonous mushrooms and died.'

'Oh, how tragic! What about your second husband?'

'He ate poisonous mushrooms too and died.'

'Oh, how terrible! I'm almost afraid to ask you about your third husband.'

'He died of a broken neck.'

'A broken neck?'

'He wouldn't eat the mushrooms.'

A young couple, just married, were in their hotel honeymoon suite on their wedding night. As they undressed for bed the husband, who was a big burly man, tossed his pants to his bride and said, 'Here, put these on.'

She put them on and the waist was twice the size of her body. 'I can't wear your pants,' she said.

'That's right!' said the husband, 'And don't you forget it. I'm the one who wears the pants in this family!'

With that she flipped him her panties and said, 'Try these on.' He tried them on and found he could only get them on as far as his kneecap.

He said, 'Hell, I can't get into your panties!'

She said, 'That's right and that's the way it's going to be until your attitude changes!'

Seems an elderly gentleman had serious hearing problems for a number of years. He went to the doctor and the doctor was able to have him fitted for a set of hearing aids that allowed the gentleman to hear 100 per cent.

Down the pub a mate says to him, 'Your hearing is perfect. Your family must be really pleased that you can hear again.'

To which the gentleman said, 'Oh, I haven't told my family yet. I just sit around and listen to the conversations. I've changed my will three times!'

After a night at the pub, as the couple was driving home, the woman asks her husband, 'Honey, has anyone ever told you how handsome, sexy and irresistible to women you are?'

The flattered husband said, 'No, dear they haven't.'

The wife yells, 'Then what the heck gave you that idea!'

A Welshman, a Scot and an Irishman are sitting in a pub a couple of days after Christmas.

The Welshman asks, 'What did you give your wife for Christmas?'

The Scot replies, 'A diamond ring and a pair of gloves.'

'Why the gloves?' asks Taffy.

'Well, if she doesn't like the ring, she can wear the gloves to cover it,' he replied.

'I got mine a necklace and a polo-neck sweater,' Taffy replied.

'If she doesn't like the necklace, she can wear the polo-neck sweater to cover it.'

'Perfectly logical,' agrees the Scot.

They then ask of the Irishman, 'What did you buy your wife for Christmas?'

The Irishman replied, 'I got her a handbag and a vibrator'

'That's an odd combination, why those two items?' says Taffy.

'Well, if she doesn't like the handbag, she can get screwed!'

The young couple's marriage was not going very well. They went for a night out at the pub to loosen up and talk about it.

'You never cry out when you are having an orgasm,' complained the husband.

'How would you know,' she replied. 'You're never there!'

Two blokes are finishing their drinks one afternoon. 'Shit,' said the first bloke, 'I'm going to down this and as soon as I get home, I'm gonna rip the wife's knickers off!'

'What's the rush?' his mate asked.

'The bloody elastic in the legs is killing me,' the bloke replied.

A guy goes over to his friend's house, rings the bell and the wife answers. 'Hi, is Tony home?'

'No, he went down the pub to buy some more beer.'

'Well, you mind if I wait?'

'No, come in.'

They sit down and the friend says, 'You know Nora, you have the greatest breasts I have ever seen. I'd give you 100 bucks if I could just see one.'

Nora thinks about this for a second and figures what the hell—100 bucks. She opens her robe and shows one. He promptly thanks her and throws 100 bucks on the table.

They sit there a while longer and Chris says, 'They are so beautiful I've got to see the both of them. I'll give you another 100 bucks if I could just see the both of them together.'

Nora thinks about this and thinks what the hell, opens her robe and gives Chris a nice long look. Chris thanks her, throws another 100 bucks on the table and then says he can't wait any longer and leaves.

A while later Tony arrives back from the pub with a slab and his wife says, 'You know, your weird friend Chris came over.'

Tony thinks about this for a second and says, 'Well, did he drop off the 200 bucks he owes me?'

You and your husband don't seem to have an awful lot in common,' said the new tenant's neighbour over a beer. 'Why on earth did you get married?'

'I suppose it was the old business of "opposites attract,"' was the reply. 'He wasn't pregnant and I was.'

Get this,' said the bloke to his mates down the pub, 'Last night while I was down here having a few drinks with you guys, a burglar broke into my house.'

'Did he get anything?' his mates asked.

'Yeah, a broken jaw, six teeth knocked out and a pair of broken nuts. The wife thought it was me coming home drunk.'

A man decided that it was time to teach his son how to say prayers.

After the kid had learned them well enough to say on his own, Dad told him that he could also choose someone special and ask for God's blessing for that person.

The first night the little boy said his prayers, he ended with 'And God, please bless my puppy.' However, the next morning the little dog ran out the door and was killed by a car.

That night the little kid asked God to bless his cat. And, sure enough, the next morning the cat slipped out and took on the biggest dog in the neighbourhood and lost.

When the kid asked God to bless his goldfish, the fish was found floating upside down on the top.

That night the little kid ended with, 'God, please give an extra special blessing to my father.'

The father couldn't sleep. He couldn't eat breakfast in the morning. He was afraid to drive to work. He couldn't get any work done because he was petrified. Finally quitting time came and he went down the pub, consumed six whiskeys, expecting to drop dead any minute.

When he arrived home, the house was a mess. His wife was lying on the couch still dressed in her robe. The dishes from breakfast were still on the table and the father was furious.

He yelled at his wife, telling her that he had had the worst day of his life and she hadn't even gotten dressed.

She looked at him and said, 'Shut up! My day was worse. The mailman had a heart attack on our front porch!'

THEN THERE WAS . . .

Then there was this guy who walks out of a bar on the moon, complaining 'The drinks were okay but there is just no atmosphere.'

Then there was the publican who tells some early patrons that the bar won't be open for another hour.
And then asks if they'd care for a drink while they wait.

Then there were the three turtles having a beer at their local. One of them says, 'Looks like we're out of cash. Might have to go to the bank.'
None of them volunteer for the mission, so they draw straws. The loser, disgruntled, departs.
About three months later, one of the turtles at the bar says to the other, 'Hey, Walter's beer's a bit flat, maybe we should share it.'
Just as he suggests this a voice at the door yells, 'You touch that beer and I won't go to the bank.'

Then there was a man drowning his sorrows at the Bridgewater Inn. The barman asks what the matter is. The man looks up from his beer and explains, 'I was out fishing and missed the birth of my twins.'
'Ah that's rough,' says the barman, 'But hey, you've got their whole life ahead of you.'
The sorry man continues, 'That's not the worst of it. Y'see my brother was at the birth and, because it's an Italian tradition for the father to decide on the names of his newborn, my brother did the honours.'
'Ah well, a name is just a name,' the barman says.
'Yes, true, but my brother is a bit of a dickhead.'

'So what did he name them.'
'Well he named the girl Denise.'
'Well, that's a nice a name. What about the boy?'
'He named him Denephew.'

Not forgetting the courier who parks his van outside the pub and goes in for a beer . . . The bloke next to him at the bar asks, 'What's in the van?'

The courier replies, 'A bunch of "Then There Was" joke books.'

'Oh. Are they funny?'

'I dunno,' says the courier, 'It's all in the delivery.'

A . . . WALKS INTO A BAR

A bull walks into a bar and the barman says, 'Ah, the china shop is down the road.'

A joke walks into a bar and says to the barman, 'What are you laughing at?'

A guy in a strange town walks into a bar.
He doesn't realise he's in a gay bar. He takes a seat and says to the man next to him, 'Can I bum a fag?'

A scull walks into a bar. He takes a seat and the barfly next to him starts to chat.

'G'day. I used to come here when I was 15,' rambles the barfly.

'Y'see my family's always lived round these parts. You wouldn't believe how much it's changed around here. New shops, new streets, new folk movin' here every bloody week. Sometimes I just don't know why I bother sticking around, some sort of attachment, I guess, you know that feeling? . . . Do ya? . . . '

The scull looks up from his drink.

'Sorry? What was that? You know me mate, in one ear out the other.'

A dwarf walks into a bar and he slips over a piece of shit on the floor. He walks off thinking nothing of it.

A few minutes later a huge man walks in and falls over

the same piece of shit, the little dwarf shouts out, 'I just did that.'

And so the big man kills him.

A wall walks into a pub, sits at the bar and orders a drink. Soon enough he notices a lovely looking wall at the other end of the bar and he says, 'Hey baby, how 'bout me and you go meet in the corner.'

J upiter walks into a bar and asks for the longest, coldest beer in the place.

The barman enquires, 'Bit thirsty mate?'

To which Jupiter replies, 'Hell, yeah . . . it's been a long day.'

A guy walks into a bar. There's a horse behind the bar serving drinks.

The guy is staring at the horse, when the horse says, 'Hey buddy? What are you staring at? Haven't you ever seen a horse serving drinks before?'

The guy says, 'No, it's not that . . . it's just that I never thought the iguana would sell the place.'

A dyslexic walks into a bra . . .

A ball rolls into a bar and bounces up onto a stool next to a friend. The friend says, 'C'mon mate. Your round.'

A pigeon, a koala, a nun, an Arab and an ice-cream walk into a bar and the barman says, 'This is gotta be the weirdest bloody joke I've ever been in.'

A déjà vu walks into a bar and the barman looks at him for a minute and says, 'Haven't I seen you before?'

LOGICAL
EXPLANATIONS

Every night, Frank would go down to the liquor store, get a six pack, bring it home and drink it while he watched TV.

One night, as he finished his last beer, the doorbell rang. He stumbled to the door and found a six foot cockroach standing there. The bug grabbed him by the collar and threw him across the room, then left.

The next night, after he finished his fourth beer, the doorbell rang. He walked slowly to the door and found the same huge cockroach standing there. The big bug punched him in the stomach, then left.

The next night, after Frank finished his first beer, the doorbell rang again. The same six foot cockroach was standing there. This time Frank was kneed in the groin and hit behind the ear as he doubled over in pain. Then the big bug left.

The fourth night Frank didn't drink at all. The doorbell rang. The cockroach was standing there. The bug beat the snot out of Frank and left him in a heap on the living room floor.

The following day, Frank went to see his doctor. He explained events of the preceding four nights. 'I thought it might be the drink. But he belted me when I didn't have a beer. What can I do?' Frank pleaded.

'Not much,' the doctor replied. 'There's just a nasty bug going around.'

Shaaayyyy, buddy, what's a Breathalyser?' asked a drunk of his barman.

'That's a bag that tells you when you've drunk too much,' answered the barman.

'Ah hell, whaddya know? I've been married to one of those for years.'

Bob, a travelling salesman, arrives at a small town late in the day, walks into the local bar, sits down and orders up a beer.

After a few moments, someone stands up and shouts, '28!' and the entire bar bursts into hysterical laughter.

Bob thinks this is strange, but goes back to his beer.

A few moments later someone else stands up and yells, '33!' Once again, the bar bursts into fits of laughter. Some are rolling on the floor.

Bob shakes his head and goes back to his beer.

Soon, a third man stands up and shouts, 'Four!' Again, everyone in the bar laughs, some uncontrollable in their mirth.

The completely confused Bob summons the bartender and asks what the hell all the laughing is about.

The bartender replies, 'See, pal, we're such a small town that everyone knows everyone and all of their jokes. So, to make life easier we catalogued all of our gags. Instead of telling the whole joke, we just shout out its number and everyone knows what joke it is and we laugh.'

Bob listens carefully, nods and sits down. More people stand up and shout numbers and eventually Bob cannot stand it any longer. Well-known as the life of the party back home, he has to join in.

Bob stands up and shouts, '41!'

Nobody laughs. There is stony silence. Bob sits down, shamefaced and embarrassed.

He summons up the bartender and says, 'What happened? No-one laughed.'

The bartender shakes his head and says, 'Buddy, it's not so much the joke, it's the way you tell it.'

A policeman is walking his beat when he finds a totally drunk man collapsed against a building, weeping uncontrollably and holding his car keys in his hands. He's moaning something about 'They took my car!' Seeing he is quite well dressed, the cop thinks he may have a real case of theft on his hands and proceeds to question the man.

'What are your car keys doing out?'

'My car, it was right on the end of my key and those bastards stole it! Please ossifer, get my Porsche back. My God, it was right on the end of my key! Where is it? They stole it and it was right here; right on my key!'

'Okay, okay, stand up, let's get some more information.' The policeman stands the man up and notices his penis is hanging out. 'Shit sir, your dick is hanging out, would you put that thing away!'

The man looks down, sees his prick hanging there and screams, 'Oh my God, they stole my girlfriend!'

BLONDES AND BARS

Chad went to a bar and ordered a drink.

After a few minutes, a beautiful blonde sat down next to him and started coming on to him. After a little while, she invited him back to her place.

Overcome with excitement, Chad agreed.

When they got to the bedroom, Chad exclaimed, 'Wow! A waterbed. I've never had sex on a waterbed before.'

Soon they were both naked and going at it.

The blonde stopped him and said, 'Before we go any further, don't you think you should put on some protection?'

'Good idea,' he responded and got up.

Chad walked out of the room and when he came back, he was wearing a life jacket.

Two blondes are sitting in the corner of a newly refurbished bar.

Across the wall opposite is a huge mirror, five metres long and stretching from floor to ceiling.

Glancing around the room, blonde number one suddenly spots their reflection in the mirror.

She whispers, 'Don't look now, but there's two women over there that are the spitting image of us!'

'Yes!' says the other, spotting the reflection. 'They're wearing identical clothes, makeup and everything! They're even blonde, the both of them.'

'That does it,' says the first blonde. 'I'm going to go over there and find out what this is all about. Those copycats!'

But as she starts to rise from her seat and take a step, the other says, 'Quick, sit down, one of them's coming over!'

The blonde comes home to her lodgings one night after too many champagnes in the bar.

The next morning she staggers down to breakfast, looking terrible.

The landlady looks at her, then says in a haughty voice, 'So, how do you find yourself this morning?'

'Same as yesterday,' the blonde replies.

'I just threw back the sheets and there I was . . .'

A bloke proposed a one dollar bar bet to a well endowed young blonde, that despite her dress being buttoned to the neck, he could touch her breasts without touching her clothes.

Since this didn't seem remotely possible, she was intrigued and accepted the bet.

He stepped up, cupped his hands around her breasts and squeezed firmly.

With a baffled look, the blonde said, 'Hey, you touched my clothes.'

And he replied, 'Damn. I owe you a dollar . . .'

One day while on patrol, a police officer pulled over a red sports car for speeding.

He went up to the car and asked the driver, who was a beautiful, buxom blonde, to roll down her window.

'I've pulled you over for speeding. Could I see your driver's licence?'

'What's a licence?' replied the blonde.

The officer thought she was playing dumb to get out of the fine and said, 'It's usually in your wallet.'

After fumbling in her bag for a few minutes, the driver managed to find it.

'Now may I see your registration?' asked the policeman.

'Registration? What's that?' asked the blonde.

The officer began to realise that maybe she wasn't pretending to be dumb, but that she actually was.

'It's usually on your windscreen,' said the cop impatiently.

The officer took her registration and licence details back to his car to contact headquarters to run a few checks.

After a few moments, the dispatcher came back, 'Um . . . is this woman driving a red sports car?'

'Yes,' replied the officer.

'Is she a drop dead gorgeous blonde?' asked the dispatcher.

'Uh . . . yes,' replied the cop.

'Here's what you do,' said the dispatcher. 'Give her licence back and drop your pants.'

'What? I can't do that. It's inappropriate!' exclaimed the cop.

'Trust me. Just do it,' said the dispatcher.

So the cop goes back to the car, gives the blonde back her stuff and drops his pants.

The blonde looks down and sighs, 'Oh no . . . not another breathalyser.'

A bloke walks into a pub with a crocodile on a leash and puts it up on the bar.

He turns to the amazed drinkers, 'Here's the deal. I'll open this crocodile's mouth and place my genitals inside. Then the croc will close his mouth for one minute. He'll then open his mouth and I'll remove my wedding tackle unscathed. In return for witnessing this spectacle, each of you will buy me a drink.'

After a few moments' silence the crowd murmurs approval.

The man stands up on the bar, drops his trousers and places his privates in the crocodile's mouth.

The croc closes his mouth as the crowd gasps. After a minute, the man grabs a beer bottle and raps the crocodile hard on the top of its head.

The croc opens his mouth and the man removes his genitals—unscathed as promised.

The crowd cheers and the first of his free drinks is delivered.

The man calls for silence and makes another offer. 'I'll pay anyone $1000 who's willing to give it a try.'

A hush falls over the crowd. After a while, a hand goes up at the back.

It's a blonde. 'I'll try,' she says. 'But only if you promise not to hit me on the head with the beer bottle . . .'

Derek drove his brand new Mercedes to his favourite bar and put it in the car park at the back. He went inside, where the bar was being looked after by Beverley, the regular waitress.

Beverley was a pretty blonde and as Derek walked into the bar, she happily greeted him. He bought a drink and went and sat at a table.

A few minutes later, Beverley came running up to him yelling, 'Derek! Derek! I was putting the trash out the back and just saw someone driving off with your new Mercedes!'

'Dear God! Did you try to stop him?'

'No,' she said, 'I did better than that! I got the licence plate number!'

Then there was the blonde who complains to her friend about constantly being called a dumb blonde.

Her friend tells her, 'Go do something to prove them wrong! Why don't you learn all the world capitals or something?'

The blonde thinks this is a great idea and locks herself up for two weeks studying.

The next time she is having a glass of bubbly with friends at the pub, some guy is making dumb blonde comments to her.

She gets all indignant and claims, 'I'm not a dumb blonde. In fact, I can name all the world capitals!'

The guy doesn't believe her, so she dares him to test her.

He says, 'Okay, what's the capital of Monaco?'

The blonde tosses her hair in triumph and says, 'That's easy! It's M!'

ONE OF THOSE DAYS

An old geezer is waiting for his mate at the bar. He orders a glass of shiraz.

Then he starts talking to the barman, 'You wouldn't believe the day I've had. I did four hours of work on the computer and lost the bloody lot in a blackout. Then as I'm heading upstairs I twist my ankle and go into the bathroom for a bandage and find my wife with another man. And then she has the audacity to kick me out of the house! It's terrible what the world has come to you know, I sometimes wonder if it's all worth it . . . '

Just then his mate turns up and takes a seat next to him.

'G'day buddy,' he says, 'What are you up to?'

The old geezer replies, 'Oh, just having a wine . . .'

A couple of racing cars are knocking back a few stiff drinks. They're having a great time and drinking themselves rotten.

At one o'clock the barman has to close up. One car says to the other, 'C'mon buddy, how 'bout we hit the late night bar in town?'

The other car answer, 'Nah mate, I'm gonna crash.'

After the International Beer Festival, all the brewery presidents decided to go out for a beer.

The guy from Corona sits down and says, 'Hey Senor, I would like the world's best beer, a Corona.'

The bartender dusts off a bottle from the shelf and gives it to him.

The guy from Budweiser says, 'I'd like the best beer in the world, give me 'The King Of Beers', a Budweiser.'

The bartender gives him one.

The guy from Coors says, 'I'd like the only beer made with Rocky Mountain spring water, give me a Coors.'

He gets it.

The guy from Victoria Bitter sits down and says, 'Give me a Coke.'

The bartender is a little taken aback, but gives him what he ordered.

The other brewery presidents look over at him and ask, 'Why aren't you drinking a VB?'

And the VB boss replies, 'Well, I figured if you guys aren't drinking beer, neither would I . . .'

A man's wife asks him to go to the store to buy some cigarettes.

So he walks down to the store only to find it closed. So he goes into a nearby bar to use the vending machine.

At the bar he sees a beautiful woman and starts talking to her. They have a couple of beers and one thing leads to another and they end up in her apartment.

After they've had their fun, he realises it's 3 am and says, 'Oh no, it's so late, my wife's going to kill me. Have you got any talcum powder?'

She gives him some talcum powder, which he proceeds to rub on his hands and then he goes home.

His wife is waiting for him in the doorway and she is pretty angry. 'Where the hell have you been?'

'Well, honey, it's like this. I went to the store like you asked, but they were closed. So I went to the bar to use the vending machine. I saw this great looking chick there and we had a few drinks and one thing led to another and I ended up in bed with her.'

'Oh yeah? Let me see your hands!' She sees his hands are covered with powder and says, 'You God damn liar!! You went bowling again!'

Two cannibals come into a bar and sit beside a clown having a quiet drink.

The first cannibal whacks the clown on the head and they both start eating him.

Suddenly the second cannibal looks up and says, 'Hey, do you taste something funny?'

A guy goes into the bar with a banana in his ear. He orders a drink. The bartender wants to mention the banana but doesn't.

Next day, the same guy with a banana in his ear goes to the same bar and orders a drink.

Again the bartender wants to say something about the banana but refrains.

The third day, the same guy with the same banana goes to the bar and orders a drink.

As the bartender serves the man he can't stand it any more.

He says to the guy, 'Hey buddy, it's none of my business, but you know you got a banana in your ear?

The guy replies, 'Sorry pal, but I can't hear you. I've got a banana in my ear.'

POLICE

A young man was pulled over on the Hume Highway by a policeman for speeding. The officer stepped out of his cop car, adjusted his sunglasses and swaggered up to the young man's window. 'What the hell are you driving so fast for boy? Let me see your licence.'

The young man handed over his licence.

Then the officer noticed that the back seat of the car was full of large knives. The officer said, 'Tell me boy, why you got them knives on that there back seat?'

The young man replied, 'Well sir, I'm a juggler.'

The officer spat and then he said, 'A juggler, well you don't say. Boy, put your hands on the boot of your car, you're going to jail!'

The young man pleaded with the officer not to take him to jail.

He offered to prove to the officer that he was a juggler by way of demonstration.

He said, 'You can even hold me at gunpoint while I juggle for you.'

The officer reluctantly allowed him to prove his point while he pulled out his pistol and held him at gunpoint.

Five kilometres down the road at Joe's Tavern, Bazza was drinking it up with Whacker.

Bazza soon left and got into his old, rusty Ute. He proceeded down the road trying his best to stay on the right side.

All of a sudden he spotted the most unbelievable sight of his life! He drove to the nearest phone booth and dialled the number for Joe's Tavern and asked for his buddy, Whacker.

When Whacker got on the phone, Bazza said, 'Whatever you do when you leave the pub, don't go north up the Hume. The cops are giving a sobriety test that nobody can pass!'

Two police officers saw this old woman staggering down the street.

Stopping her, they can tell she has had far too much to drink and instead of taking her to jail they decide to just drive her home.

They load her into the police cruiser, one of the officers gets in the back with the drunk woman.

As they drove through the streets they kept asking the woman where she lived, all she would say as she stroked the officer's arm is, 'You're passionate.'

They drove a while longer and asked again, but again the same response as she stroked his arm, 'You're passionate.'

The officers were getting a little upset so they stopped the car and said to the woman, 'Look we have driven around this city for two hours and you still haven't told us where you live.'

She replied, 'I keep trying to tell you, your passin' it!'

UP HERE FOR THINKING . . .

A man walks into a pub with a neck brace around his neck. He asks for a pint. The bartender gives him one.

Then the man asks, 'Who's in the lounge?'

The bartender replies, 'Fifteen people playing darts.'

The man says, 'Get them a pint too.'

Then he asks, 'Who's upstairs?'

The bartender replies, '150 people at the disco.'

The man says, 'Get them a drink too.'

The bartender says, 'That will be $328 please.'

The man says, 'Sorry but I haven't got that much money on me.'

The bartender says, 'If you were at the pub a mile from here, they would have broke your neck.'

The man says, 'I've already been there.'

A sign in a bar read, 'Those drinking to forget, please pay in advance . . .'

A man walks into a bar pulling a heavy chain. The bartender asks the man what he could get him and why the man was pulling that chain around.

The man answered, 'Hey! you ever tried pushing one of these things!'

A gay guy walks into a bar and says 'Bartender, give me a brewskie.'

The bartender says, 'We don't serve your kind here.'

The gay continues, 'I'll just sit in the corner and drink my beer and won't say anything.'

The bartender says, 'Well, all right!' and pours a beer.

A while later a cowboy walks in and says, 'Bartender give me a beer! I'm so thirsty, I could lick the sweat off a cow's balls.'

A voice is heard from the corner. 'Moo!'

JUST FOR FUN

An elderly couple had dinner at another couple's house and after eating, the wives left the table and went into the kitchen.

The two elderly gentlemen were talking and one said, 'Last night we went out to a new pub and it was really great. I would recommend it very highly.'

The other man said, 'What's the name of the pub?'

The first man knits his brow in obvious concentration and finally says to his companion, 'Ah, what is the name of that red flower you give to someone you love?'

His friend replies, 'A carnation?'

'No. No. The other one,' the man says.

His friend offers another suggestion, 'The poppy?'

'Nah,' growls the man, 'You know the one that is red and has thorns.'

His friend says, 'Do you mean a rose?'

'Yes, yes that's it. Thank you!' the first man says.

He then turns towards the kitchen and yells, 'Hey, Rose, what's the name of that pub we went to last night . . .?'

A little boy was found wandering at a large shopping mall. He approached a uniformed policeman and said, 'I've lost my dad! He's in a tavern here somewhere.'

The cop asked, 'What's he like?'

The little boy replied, 'Beer and women with big tits.'

There is a Navy guy and a Marine in the pub washroom. The Marine goes to leave without washing up.

The sailor catches up with him later and says, 'In the Navy, they teach us to wash our hands.'

The Marine replies, 'In the Marines, they teach us not to pee on ours!!'

Tom walks out of a bar, swaying back and forth with a key in his hand. A cop on the beat sees him and approaches.

'Can I help you, fella?' asks the cop.

'Yes! Somebody stole my car!' Tom replies.

The cop asks, 'Okay, where was your car the last time you saw it?'

'It was at the end of this key!' Tom replies.

At this point, the cop looks down and sees Tom's penis hanging out of his trousers.

So he asks Tom, 'Hey buddy, come on now, are you aware that you're exposing yourself?'

Tom looks down sadly and moans, 'Oh God . . . they got my girlfriend too!'

After many gin and tonics to bolster her spirits, a lady leaves the pub and walks into her doctor's office screaming.

She yells, 'Doctor, Doctor my breasts are hairy! What do I do?'

The doctor asks, 'Well, how long does the hair grow?'

The lady replies, 'From here to my penis, but that's a different story!'

A baby seal walks into a club. I'll repeat myself. A baby seal walks into a club.

An older man wearing a stovepipe hat, a waistcoat and a phoney beard sat down at a bar and ordered a drink. As the bartender set it down, he asked, 'Going to a party?'

'Yeah, a costume party,' the man answered, 'I'm supposed to come dressed as my "love life".'

'But you look like Abe Lincoln,' protested the barkeep.

'That's right. My last four scores were seven years ago.'

THE PEOPLE YOU MEET . . .

A 90-year-old man meets up with a doctor in the pub. 'I reckon I would be one of the best preserved men for my age that you have met in your medical career,' the old man says.

'I have an 18-year old bride who is pregnant with my child. What do you think about that?'

The doctor considered his question for a minute and then says, 'I have an elderly friend who is a hunter and never misses a season. One day when he was going out in a bit of a hurry, he accidentally picked up his umbrella instead of his gun. When he got to the creek, he saw a rabbit sitting beside the stream. He raised his umbrella and went, "bang, bang" and the rabbit fell dead. What do you think of that?'

The 90-year-old said, 'I'd say somebody else killed that rabbit.'

The doctor replied, 'My point exactly . . .'

A lady walks into a bar and says, 'Barkeep, gimme a martooni.' The bartender goes back and fixes her a martini.

She downs it and says, 'Barkeep, gimme another martooni.'

So he goes back and fixes her another martini.

She downs that and just sits there and doesn't say anything.

Finally after about ten minutes the bartender says, 'Would you like another?' She says, 'Oh, no, I got this terrible heartburn.'

The bartender says, 'Okay, there are three things wrong here. Number one, it's martini, not martooni. Number two, it's bartender, not barkeep and number three, you're not having heartburn, your left boob's flopped in the ash tray.'

A Frenchman, an Englishman, an American and a lawyer were standing around the bar.

The Frenchman offered everyone some of his baguette, then threw the rest in the rubbish can, saying, 'Don't worry—we have plenty of those where I come from.'

The Englishman offered everyone a crumpet, then threw the rest out, saying, 'Don't worry—we have plenty of those where I come from.'

Then the American threw the lawyer in the trash, saying . . .

A woman walks into a restaurant and sits down.
As she bends down to reach into her purse for her wallet, she farts loudly with the waiter right behind her.

She sits abruptly back up, glares at the waiter and shouts, 'Stop that!'

To which the waiter replies, 'Sure, which way did it go?'

A n office executive was interviewing a blonde over a pub lunch for an assistant position and wanted to find out a little about her personality.

'If you could have a conversation with anyone, alive or dead, who would it be?'

'I'd have to say the living one . . .'

A man meets a bloke in the bar.
After a while, they get chatting and he finds out that his new-found friend is a doctor.

He says, 'Look, I know that you're off duty, but I was just wondering . . .'

'Yeah, sure,' says the doctor, 'You don't seem such a bad guy, what's the problem?'

They go into the toilet, where the bloke shows the doctor his penis.

It has a red ring around it.

The doctor rustles around in his bag and gives him an ointment to rub on the problem area.

A few days later, they meet in the bar again.

'It's all cleared up!' the man reports. 'But what was that medication you gave me?'

'Lipstick remover . . .'

OH, BY THE WAY . . .

A man and his pet giraffe walk into a bar and start having a few quiet drinks.

As the night goes on, they get pretty drunk.

The giraffe finally passes out near the pool tables and the man decides to go home.

As the man is leaving, he's approached by the barman who says, 'Hey, you're not gonna leave that lyin' here, are ya?'

'Humph,' says the man, 'That's not a lion, it's a giraffe.'

A young punk comes into a bar and sits down directly across from an old man.

The young punk has spiked green, purple and orange hair.

His clothing is a tattered mix of leather rags. His entire face and body are covered with piercings and his earrings are big, bright red, yellow and green feathers.

The old man stares at the young punk as they quietly consume a few drinks.

Finally, the punk looks across at the old man and yells, 'What are you looking at, old man! Didn't you do anything wild when you were young?'

Without missing a beat, the old man replies, 'Yeah. Back when I was very young and in the Navy, I got really drunk in Singapore and had sex with a parrot . . . I thought you might be my son.'

W hen Mozart passed away, he was buried in a churchyard. A couple of days later, the town drunk was walking through the cemetery and heard some strange noise coming from the area where Mozart was buried.

Terrified, the drunk ran and got the town magistrate to come and listen to it.

When the magistrate arrived, he bent his ear to the grave, listened for a moment and said, 'Ah, yes, that's Mozart's Ninth Symphony, being played backwards.'

He listened a while longer and said, 'There's the Eighth Symphony and it's backwards, too. Most puzzling.'

So the magistrate kept listening. 'There's the Seventh . . . the Sixth . . . the Fifth . . .'

Suddenly the realisation of what was happening dawned on the magistrate. He stood up and announced to the crowd that had gathered in the cemetery, 'My fellow citizens, there's nothing to worry about. It's just Mozart decomposing.'

A panda bear walks into a pub and orders a sandwich. When he receives the sandwich, he eats it and then shoots the waiter and leaves the restaurant.

A policeman sees the panda and tells him he just broke the law. The panda bear tells the policeman that he's innocent and, if he didn't believe him, to look in the dictionary. The policeman gets a dictionary and looks up 'Panda bear'.

It says, 'Panda Bear—Eats shoots and leaves.'

I met my wife at a singles bar.'
'Really?'

'I thought she was home with the kids.'

A man, whose level of drunkenness was bordering on the absurd, stood up to leave a bar and fell flat on his face.

'Maybe all I need is some fresh air,' thought the man as he crawled outside.

He tried to stand up again, but fell face first into the mud.

'Screw it,' he thought. 'I'll just crawl home.'

The next morning, his wife found him on the doorstep asleep.

'You went out drinking last night, didn't you?' she said.

'Uh, yes,' he said sheepishly. 'How did you know?'
'You left your wheelchair at the bar again.'

Q: What is the mating call of a blonde?
A: 'I'm soooo drunk.'

THE GLORIES
OF AGE

Two retired professors were vacationing with their wives at a hotel in the Catskills. They were sitting on the veranda of the local hotel one summer evening, watching the sun set.

The history professor asked the psychology professor, 'Have you read Marx?'

To which the professor of psychology replied, 'Yes and I think it's these pesky wicker chairs.'

Jack and Betty are celebrating their fiftieth wedding anniversary with a nice dinner and a few wines at the pub.

'Betty, I was wondering—have you ever cheated on me?'

'Oh Jack, why would you ask such a question now? You don't want to ask that question . . .'

'Yes, Betty, I really want to know. Please.'

'Well, all right. Yes, three times.'

'Three? When were they?'

'Well, Jack, remember when you were 35 years old and you really wanted to start the business on your own and no bank would give you a loan? Remember how one day the bank president himself came over to the house and signed the loan papers, no questions asked?'

'Oh, Betty, you did that for me! I respect you even more than ever, that you would do such a thing for me! So, when was number two?'

'Well, Jack, remember when you had that last heart attack and you were needing that very tricky operation and no surgeon would touch you? Remember how Dr DeBakey came all the way up here, to do the surgery himself and then you were in good shape again?'

'I can't believe it! Betty, I love that you should do such a thing for me, to save my life! I couldn't have a more wonderful wife. To do such a thing, you must really love me darling. I couldn't be more moved. When was number three?'

'Well, Jack, remember a few years ago, when you really wanted to be president of the golf club and you were 17 votes short . . .?'

STRANGE EVENTS

Some Guinness was spilled on the bar room floor and the pub was closed for the night. Out from his hole, crept a little brown mouse and stood in the pale moonlight.

He lapped up the frothy brew from the floor and back on his haunches he sat.

And all night long you could hear him roar, 'Bring on the God damn cat!'

Two donkeys walk into a bar and the first donkey says to the bartender 'I'll have a pot of VB please.'

And the second donkey says, 'Hee haw, hee haw, he always orders that.'

A blackout walks into a bar, sits down, pops a cigarette in his mouth and says to the barman, 'Got a light?'

JFK walks into a bar and the barman asks, 'What'll it be? Wine? Beer? A cocktail?'

JFK thinks for a moment and says, 'I'll just take a shot.'

A guy sits in a pub and is tossing up between a lager and a glass of chardonnay.

All of a sudden he notices a ghost fly above his head.

He looks around and sees another couple of ghosts loitering in the corner.

As the barman approaches he's followed by yet another ghostly looking figure.

The man, quite shaken, asks the barman what the hell is going on to which the barman just points to a blackboard that reads, 'beer, wine and spirits.'

A guy sits at a bar and notices a clown next to him giggling. He looks around and sees two other clowns laughing in a corner.

He looks around further and realises everywhere he looks, there are laughing clowns. Bemused, he asks the barman, 'What's going on in here?'

The barman replies, 'It's happy hour.'

A hammer walks into a bar and asks for an ale.

A cow walks into a bar and asks in a very cow-sounding voice, 'Can I have a beer please?'

The barman replies, 'Sorry, but you're a cow. We can't serve you beer.'

The disgruntled cow protests, 'But I'm thirsty, where am I supposed to get a drink?'

To which the barman replies, 'You'll have to try an udder bar.'

I was sitting at a bar when someone yelled at me, 'You're as soft as strawberry jam!'

I thought I'd take that as a condiment.

A snake slithers into a bar and the barman says, 'So, what's your poison?'

IT'S HOW YOU SAY IT

Two men are talking in the bar sharing their sob stories. One man says, 'I had the worst Freudian slip the other day.'

The other man responds, 'What is a Freudian slip?'

'You know, it's when you mean to say one thing, but you say something else that reveals what you are really thinking about. Like the other day I was at the airport and this really beautiful lady was helping me. And instead of asking her for "two tickets to Pittsburgh," I asked her for "two Pickets to Tittsburgh".'

The second replies, 'Oh, now I know what you are talking about. It's like the other day when I was having breakfast with my wife. I wanted her to pass me the orange juice and instead I said, "YOU RUINED MY LIFE BITCH!"'

There was once a lemur called Faizal.
Faizal was no ordinary lemur.

In fact, instead of wasting his time sitting around with the other lemurs, Faizal would spend his days and nights drinking at the local pub.

Faizal became a legend, he would sit at the bar and tell stories of lemur legend while everybody bought him drinks.

Unfortunately, our friend Faizal had a bit of a temper and became involved in a horrible dispute one night.

One thing led to another and Faizal was horribly dismembered by a young lout with a flick-knife.

His bloodied corpse lay on the pavement outside the pub and his severed fluffy tail lay in the gutter. He was pronounced dead at the scene.

So disheartened were the pub's patrons that they commissioned a plaque in Faizal's honour.

They had his cute fluffy tail mounted to a mahogany plaque, which they hung above the bar.

One Sunday evening after closing time, there was a knock on the pub door.

The bartender opened the door and who should be there, but a ghostly image of the deceased Faizal

'Holy mother of Jesus,' said the barman, 'It's Faizal.'

The spirit lifted a ghostly finger and pointed towards the plaque above the bar and then towards his own severed stump where a tail should have been.

'Ah,' said the barman, 'You want your tail back, don't you ?'

The ghostly lemur nodded.

'Sorry,' said the barman, 'We don't retail spirits on a Sunday . . .'

Two smart fellows were in a pub. They called the owner over and asked him to settle an argument.

'Are there two stubbies in a long neck?' asked one.

'Yep,' confirmed the owner.

They moved back along the bar and soon the barmaid asked for their order.

'Two stubbies please, miss and they are on the house.'

The barmaid doubted that her boss would be so generous so one of the fellows called out to the owner at the other end of the bar, 'You did say two stubbies, didn't you?'

'That's right,' he called back, 'Two stubbies.'

MOTHER-IN-LAW

Two blokes are sitting in the pub, pondering their lives.
'Is it possible to kill a mother-in-law with newspaper?' one says.

'Yes', replies the other, 'But only if you wrap an iron in it . . .'

A newlywed farmer and his wife were visited by her mother. They took her to the pub to have a few drinks.

But even after a few liberal pints of lager, she was insistent on inspecting the place.

The farmer had genuinely tried to be friendly to his new mother-in-law, hoping that theirs would be a non-antagonistic relationship.

All to no avail. She nagged them at every opportunity, demanding changes, offering unwanted advice and generally making life unbearable to the farmer and his new bride.

During a forced inspection of the barn, the farmer's mule suddenly reared up and kicked the mother-in-law in the head, killing her instantly.

It was a shock to all, no matter what they thought of her demanding ways.

At the funeral service a few days later, the farmer stood near the casket and greeted folks as they walked by.

The pastor noticed that whenever a woman would whisper something to the farmer, he would nod his head yes and say something.

Whenever a man walked by and whispered to the farmer, however, he would shake his head no and mumble a reply.

Very curious as to this bizarre behaviour, the pastor later asked the farmer what that was all about.

The farmer replied, 'The women would say, "What a terrible tragedy" and I would nod my head and say "Yes, it was." The men would ask, "Can I borrow that mule?" and I would shake my head and say, "I can't. It's all booked up for a year".'

A big-game hunter went on safari with his wife and mother-in-law. One evening, while still deep in the jungle, the wife awoke to find her mother gone. Rushing to her husband, she insisted on them both trying to find her mother.

The hunter picked up his rifle, took a swig of whiskey and started to look for her. In a clearing not far from the camp, they came upon a chilling sight. The mother-in-law was backed up against a thick, impenetrable bush and a large male lion stood facing her.

The wife cried, 'What are we going to do?'

'Nothing,' said the husband.

'The lion got himself into this mess. Let him get himself out of it.'

A man returned home from a big night on the grog down the pub and went straight up to the bedroom.

He found his wife with the sheet pulled over her head, fast asleep. Not to be denied, the horny husband crawled under the sheet and proceeded to make love to her.

Afterward, as he hurried downstairs for something to eat, he was startled to find breakfast on the table and his wife pouring coffee.

'How'd you get down here so fast?' he asked. 'We were just making love!'

'Oh my God,' his wife gasped, 'That's my mother up there! She came over early and had complained of having a headache. I told her to lie down for awhile.'

Rushing upstairs, the wife ran to the bedroom.

'Mother, I can't believe this happened. Why didn't you say something?'

The mother-in-law huffed, 'I haven't spoken to that jerk for 15 years and I wasn't about to start now!'

OH, I SAY . . .

A tourist arrived in New Zealand, hired a car and set off for the outback. On his way he saw a bloke having sex with a sheep.

Deeply horrified, he pulled up at the nearest pub and ordered a straight scotch. Just as he was about to throw it back, he saw a bloke with one leg masturbating furiously at the bar.

'What the hell!' the tourist cried, 'What the hell's going on here? I've been here one hour and I've seen a bloke shagging a sheep and now some bloke's wanking himself off in the bar!'

'Fair dinkum, mate,' the bartender told him, 'You can't expect a man with only one leg to catch a sheep.'

Macka and Jacka were having a beer, when Macka told Jacka that he'd broken up with his missus.

Jacka asked what the problem had been.

'Sickness,' said Macka.

'I didn't know either of you were sick,' said Jacka.

'Oh, it was me,' said Jacka, 'I was bloody sick of her.'

A priest was sitting at the bar of a hotel waiting for Mother Superior when a prostitute approached him and said, 'How 'bout it big Daddy, only 30 bucks a trick.'

The priest, a little stunned, explains he is waiting for a friend. Mother Superior arrives a little later and the priest asks her, 'Mother, what's a trick?' To which she replies, 'Thirty bucks.'

Three men get so blind at a pub, they decide to take one of the rooms upstairs to crash for the night.

In the morning as they sit down at the bar for a greasy breakfast the man who slept on the right side of the bed says,

'I had the weirdest dream last night. Someone was jerking me off.'

The man who slept on the left side chips in, 'Struth mate, I had the same dream!'

'Not me,' says the bloke who slept in the middle, 'I had a lovely dream that I was skiing.'

A traveller walks into a hotel and asks for a room for the night. The manager explains that the place is full.

The traveller pleads for somewhere to kip, as it's late and there's nowhere else for miles.

The manager thinks for a moment and says, 'Well, there is a spare bed in old Charlie Donegan's room, but he snores like a chainsaw and you probably won't be able to sleep.'

The traveller says he'll take the bed and give it a try nonetheless.

In the morning the traveller bounces downstairs for breakfast bright eyed and bushy tailed.

The manager is curious. 'So you slept alright then?'

'Sure,' replied the traveller.

'Snoring not a problem for you then?'

'Nah, when I went to bed I gave Charlie a big snog on the lips and said "See you in the morning, gorgeous," and he was up all night keeping an eye on me.'

Two old biddies, Beryl and Gladys, are at a bar sipping a sherry when the town drunk saunters up, opens his trench coat and flashes the ladies.

Poor old Beryl had a stroke . . . but Gladys couldn't quite reach.

An old geezer sits at a bar, when this monkey jumps up on the bar, cracks an egg on his head and sticks a sausage in it.

The geezer says to the barman, 'What's the deal with the monkey?'

Barman replies, 'He thinks he's a griller.'

A morbid looking bloke at a bar looks so glum the barman feels he should try to cheer him up. 'What's up lad, you look a tad down in the dumps.'

'Oh, mate. It's terrible. I've got some terrible disease. My dick's all orange and I reckon it might drop off.'

The barman is horrified and asks the bloke if he's been to a doctor.

'Nah. I'm unemployed and can't really afford the medical bill.'

The barman is concerned. 'Well how did you get this thing? Have you been rooting around a lot?'

'Not at all,' replies the bloke. 'All I do all day is stay home, watch porno movies and eat Cheezels.'

N eil Armstrong is trying to have a quiet drink at his local bar. A couple of young nerds come up to him and ask for his autograph.

But a drunk dickhead next to him asks rudely, 'So, what's so bloody special about you then?'

To which Neil politely replies, 'Actually, I was the first man on the moon.'

The drunk gets a bit shirty and continues to boast, 'Yeah, well NASA is now preparing to put the first man on the sun and I've been chosen to be the man.'

Armstrong is getting impatient but humours the drunk a little longer, 'Well, that's ridiculous. Any spacecraft would burn up instantly within any vicinity of the sun.'

'Ha!' the drunk guffaws, 'You moron. We're going at night.'

OCCUPATIONS

A drunk, a painter and a politician are sitting at a bar when the drunk tells the other two how, since he's been taking Viagra, he's always getting laid.

The painter says he wouldn't mind trying it, so the drunk pulls the pills from his pocket, gives one to the painter and one to the politician.

The painter takes his pill and there's immediately a spring in his step and a bulge in his pants.

The politician pops his and begins to grow taller . . .

A council worker ambles lazily into a bar. He sits down next to one of the regulars. The regular says, 'You guys remind me of sperm.'

'Sperm?' asks the council worker, mystified, 'Why sperm?'

'Only one in a million of you does any work.'

A horse and cart, with the farmer holding the reins, come crashing through the doors of a bar.

The horse swings around so the wagon is lined up alongside the bar.

The barman says to the farmer, 'Struth, did you have to come barging in here like that? Look at the damage you've done. You can't be that desperate for a drink.'

'Oh, I don't want a drink,' the farmer says. 'I'm on the wagon.'

A farmer walks into a bar looking a bit dejected.
Bruno the barman asks him what's troubling him.

The farmer explains, 'Oh, it's the dildo farm . . . we're having real problems with the squatters.'

The cowhand got paid on Friday and immediately rode into town and proceeded to get thoroughly shit faced.

A couple of pals decided to play a trick on him.

They snuck out, turned his horse around and went back to join the hapless for a few more rounds.

The next morning, when the alarm clock and a glass of cold water in the face failed to have the slightest effect, the cowhand's wife started shaking him by the shoulders and screaming, 'Tex, get up! You have to hit the goddamn trail, you've got work to do.'

'Can't,' mumbled Tex. 'Too beat. Too tired. Can't even lift my head.'

'Get the hell up!' she screamed in his ear. 'I've seen you this hungover a thousand times.'

'Last night was different,' said the wretched fellow. 'Some son of a bitch cut my horse's head off and I had to pull him all the way home with my finger in his windpipe!'

Bob woke up after the annual office Christmas party with a pounding headache, cotton-mouthed and utterly unable to recall the events of the preceding evening.

After a trip to the bathroom, he made his way downstairs, where his wife put some coffee in front of him.

'Louise,' he moaned, 'Tell me what happened last night. Was it as bad as I think?'

'Even worse,' she said, her voice oozing scorn. 'You made a

complete ass of yourself. You succeeded in antagonising the entire board of directors and you insulted the president of the company, right to his face.'

'He's an idiot,' Bob said. 'Piss on him!'

'You did,' came the reply. 'And he fired you.'

'Well, screw him!' said Bob.

'I did,' said Louise. 'Twice. You're back at work on Monday.'

O ne day, four construction workers were in the local watering hole fighting over who had the biggest appendage.

So, all four took their dicks out and laid them on top of the bar.

They were in the process of measuring themselves when a gay man came into the tavern. As the gay guy walked up to the bar, the bartender asked him, 'What will you have?'

The gay guy replied, 'I believe that I'll have the buffet!'

A pirate walked into a bar and the bartender said, 'Hey, I haven't seen you in a while. What happened, you look terrible!'

'What do you mean? I'm fine.'

'What about that wooden leg? You didn't have that before.'

'Well', said the pirate, 'We were in a battle at sea and a cannon ball hit my leg but the Doc fixed me up and I'm fine, really.'

'Oh yeah? Well, what about that hook? The last time I saw you, you had both hands.'

'We were in another battle and we boarded the enemy ship. I was in a sword fight and my hand was cut off, but the Doc fixed me up with the hook and I feel great, really.'

'Oh,' said the bartender, 'What about that eye patch? The last time you were in here you had both eyes.'

'One day when we were at sea some birds were flying over the ship. I looked up and one of them crapped in my eye.'

'You're kidding,' said the bartender, 'You couldn't have lost an eye just from some bird crap!'

'Well, it was me first day with the hook.'

Two furniture salesmen are sitting at the bar commiserating. One says, 'Man! If I don't move some furniture this month, I'm going to lose my ass.'

The second salesman says, 'Watch your mouth! There's a lady sitting next to you. I apologise for my friend, M'am.'

The woman looks at him and says, 'That's okay. I'm a hooker. If I don't move some ass this month, I'm going to lose my furniture!'

AND FINALLY . . .

There was a bar with a sign that read 'Pianist Wanted.' So this guy walks in and says, 'I'm here for the pianist job.'

The owner says, 'Well play us a tune and if you're good enough then you've got the gig.'

So he sits down and plays a song that nearly puts the owner in tears. 'Oh, what a great song! What's it called?' the manager asks.

The piano player replies, 'It's called, The Dog with Two Dicks and my Wife's Rootin' my Brother!'

The publican is a bit taken aback. 'Um, that's a bit odd, young man, but you are so good! Play us one more tune.'

So the man plays another tune and this time the manager breaks down in tears. 'It's wonderful! What do you call that song?' he sheepishly asks.

'The Frog Takin' a Shit and the Camel with Three Humps!' the piano man replies.

The manager shakes his head and after some thought, tells him that he has the job on one condition.

'Please do not tell the customers the names of the songs you are playing,' he begs.

They shake hands and he starts playing that night.

After every song, he gets a standing ovation. The place is going wild. They're buying drinks and food like it's going out of style and the publican is beaming.

After about two hours, the piano player stands up and says, 'Ladies and gentlemen, I'm going to take a quick break and I will return to play more of my songs in a few moments.'

So he ducks into the toilet to take a quick slash, keen to get back and thrill the crowd some more.

On his way out a man passing him in the corridor says, 'Hey mate, do you know your zip's undone and your cock's hangin' out?'

'Know it?' he replies. 'I wrote it!'